PLEASE LEAVE
A LIGHT ON

BRYAN DOW

Cooper & Jones Press

ISBN: 978-0-578-20184-9

Bible quotes used from Good News Bible 1976.

Cover Photo © 2018 thinkstockphotos.com. All rights reserved - used with permission.

PRINTED IN THE UNITED STATES OF AMERICA

Warning: this book targets an adult audience that can handle adult themes even sexually explicit ones in rare cases. One must guess why? The second to last time I went to Washington DC in August of 1992 I saw two prostitutes while walking home from dinner, and there was a raunchy strip club just a few doors down from the Holiday Inn where I was staying. This book furthermore is not for the faint of heart and hits at violence, provides basis for discrimination by disability and gives justification for how and why a family has been torn apart for the past twenty-four years.

Psychiatrists, cognitive psychologists, and other mental health professionals have concluded that any of my accusations in trying to put the pieces of this puzzle together are actually hallucinations and therefore false. I guess I am a bit crazy or borderline insane, but isn't there a medication for that? Any names of people herein are either deceased or make believe. There are instances where a person's title is referenced but, then again, no official name has been designated.

Suggestions for reading this memoir include reading the "Epilogue" first.

Table of Contents

INTO THE DARK, into the night I desire the comforts of my home minus the basement and attic where fond memories exist. Having bipolar disorder has caused me to think that I can't experience those happy times again. No, this is not a book about being afraid of the dark. Rather, it is one in which I feel alive sitting at the computer desk and recollecting my post high school history up until the present day. More importantly, it is about the perspective of a man with a serious mental illness. I save the writing for another day, but it is difficult to sleep because my dog's snoring simultaneously interferes with the fog horn in the distance on Lake Michigan.

The voice of the Milwaukee Bucks and Brewers, Green Bay Packers, and Wisconsin Badgers radio station 620 AM woke me up today, so I chose to wet a line in Lake Michigan. Fishing might be my top hobby since I consider golf a sport. Numerous trails traverse the bluffs of my beloved Great Lake, and I chose to descend on one where Silver Spring Drive and Lake Drive meet in nearby Whitefish Bay. Oh, how I remember this particular hotspot. I once swam in low 50-degree water to un-snag a $3 fishing lure stuck in this underwater rocky abyss. Another time I was fishing in a nearby Big Bay Park spot where this luminiscent green, toxic slime was flowing into the lake not far from where I was trying to catch lunch. Obviously, a time in which I wish I had a trusty disposable camera!

Later that day I headed down the block from home to St. Robert's Fair. It is held the first weekend in June each year. For someone who visits Six Flags Great America every other year or so, the rides at the fair were not very interesting. Still, the dime toss is a real treat in which you can win 2-liter bottles of soda if the dime settles on the elevated glass platter. Then there is the Moon Bounce. I remember going in there one past year. I hurdled over a little girl upon exiting the ride, and it turned out that her father was the operator. He cussed me out. The scary thing about this man was that he resembled Governor Edmund Gerry Brown who ran for President back in 1992. Sure, you remember candidate Brown touting his 800 phone number and raising campaign money by selling turtlenecks with the number on it. Are you ready for a bold accusation for a man with a BA in Government? It was Brown and Clinton who gerrymandered many urban districts reaching out into the suburbs when district lines were redrawn. Eventually it was Brown that threw his support to Clinton because the former Arkansas Governor could better handle carrying or at least improving the Democrats' chances in the general election throughout the South. Call me crazy, but this was just based on personal perception. The gerrymandering impacted my home district.

My boss at the Village of Shorewood Department of Public Works offered some words of wisdom in the years leading up to my mental illness diagnosis. He told me to try to focus on the task at hand. The problem with me and my bipolar disorder previously coined the term manic depression is that it is difficult to maintain concentration or focus for long periods of time. This particular boss assigned me to rearrange and set bricks outside of the old Kohl's grocery store. The challenge existed as I was assigned to use new mortar to secure the bricks in an orderly, straight fashion. I could not get the bricks very straight, so I almost lost my job. At the time my father was serving as a village trustee, and I had my first mental health setback in 1993 at twenty years old.

The College of Wooster

I BEGAN MY undergraduate studies at the age of eighteen in northeastern Ohio at the College of Wooster in August of 1991. Why did I choose Wooster? My SAT and ACT scores kept me from being accepted at Williams and Bowdoin out East. I was wait-listed at Carleton in Minnesota. My dad had studied at Williams and thought it would be a good fit for undergrad. He had always encouraged me academically to set high goals and have high standards. I pushed myself hard especially at this stage in my academic career. Wooster was a sound academic school, and the sports teams were also strong and very competitive. The golf program lured me, and its coach was in the Hall of Fame at the collegiate level. My teammates on any given day would shoot between the upper 60's and mid 70's, so I found myself as first or second reserve. Nevertheless, you could not beat free golf at the country club or the college course. I did not have bipolar disorder yet, but I was having the hardest time trying to play solid golf while maintaining as close as possible to a 4.0 grade point average. I would literally camp out in the library and pull off all-nighters. My roommate situation was also stressful.

My roommate was also an athlete. He played second base on the baseball team. Just about everyone on my floor was an athlete of some sort. The partying was never-ending, and we had the only uncarpeted floor in Holden Hall. The football players used to slide down the hallway on mattresses with the floor covered in cheap beer. My roommate was proud of his towering collection of Budweiser cans. He absolutely adored video games and had a Sega Genesis system in our room. Unfortunately for me, he used to invite friends over to play at 3 AM. Boy was I ever pissed off! I had an 8 AM Monday, Wednesday, and Friday Introduction to Geology class with a reputation for being extremely difficult and very time-consuming. I notified my RA or resident assistant, and the three of us had a conference. The next day the RA was in the room playing video games with my roommate. About the only thing that soothed me late at night was the periodic whistling of a train in the distance. With all of the burning of midnight oil for my academic responsibility, I have no doubt that the stress from having an unreasonable roommate and rising early for golf rounds contributed to the onset of my bipolar diagnosis in the few years to come. With headstrong determination I took action and moved one floor up at semester's end where seniors lived and writing their theses consumed much of their time.

My first semester experiences living in the basement of Holden Hall did have some positive aspects. I met a guy from Philadelphia who ended up going to a lot of meals with me. He was very popular and also a chick magnet. Girls flocked to him, so I had more female companions because of him. Still, I never had the courage to ask a woman out. He was an English major- one heck of a writer who was praised highly for his essays. Today we keep in touch once per month. Back in 1999 in the spring I visited him in his current residence of Albuquerque, New Mexico. I was only there for four days, but it was enough for him to throw a wild party. Mission accomplished: I got laid and even got to take a ride to the top of the Sandia Mountains. Back then he was importing something like tea leaves from Paraguay called yerba mate. He had a website and sold various types of mate all over the US. Now he works in an economic development capacity in GIS(Geographic Information Systems). He was grateful back in those college days for me bringing Wisconsin beer like Leinenkugel's to Wooster. We were also running mates and pushed each other three or four times per week jogging the two college golf courses. At the end of our freshman year we, along with my new second semester roommate, planned and succeeded a trip to the Boundary Waters along the Minnesota/Canadian border in mid May. The lakes were not even 50 degrees, so we could not swim. We had fun canoeing, camping, fishing and hiking for four days and spent the remainder of the week fishing in central Minnesota where we had greater fishing luck.

My new roommate was from the Twin Cities, and we had a lot in common from the get-go. We were both conscientious students trying our hardest to excel in our studies. He was a sophomore psychology major while I had decided to major in political science after my first semester. We both loved to fish. On a few occasions we went to the Charles Mill Reservoir and the Turkeyfoot Lakes near campus. Never catching much most likely since we were limited to the shore, we enjoyed immersing ourselves in nature. One time he drove us forty-five minutes north to Cleveland, and we went to the movies and saw "A River Runs Through It." We had the theater to ourselves. When the school year ended we went to the Boundary Waters and central Minnesota. Both of us caught some nice fish including my small-mouth bass that was close to a college football in size. Our other buddy mostly sat in the middle of the canoe and caught very few fish.

Hard partying was not part of my lifestyle except on an occasional Friday night while at Wooster. My few friends might have consumed alcohol both weekend nights, but most of them were good students. I brought cases of Leinenkugel's beer from WI to OH, and we sculpted a beautiful pyramid using the cans. Interestingly, the pyramid was the first thing anyone would notice when leaving the library and that is where I spent my other weekend evening to alleviate the stress of the upcoming week.

Nose to the grindstone was my attitude towards academics for my undergraduate years but no more than my very first year at Wooster. My near 4.0 grade point average was pleasantly rewarded by the college and my father. I received a student-athlete t-shirt as well as a beautiful tankard that I still have today. My dad took me during the winter holiday to Panama City, FL for some golfing. I remember well the conversation we had when he took me out for an expensive seafood dinner. He asked me what happened in the two classes that I got an A- and a B+. Still, he said I was well on my way to getting into a good law school.

All in all, Wooster was a good place. The commons food was cooked by moms and grandmas that used their experience to keep my hungry body well nourished. They made homemade cookies, Belgian waffles, macaroni and cheese, chili over rice, and broccolini among my favorites.

I joined the Outdoor Club, and we went to the mountains of West Virginia for fall break during my first year. One of my fondest memories was catching a brook trout that had nine colors. I released it as I had been taught at Camp Fish back when I was in middle school. One woman on the trip hypothesized over a campfire as to how the men and women would pair up as couples. I was the odd man out with no partner although I had always been outgoing in high school and had plenty of friends of the opposite sex.

I did have a crush on a sorority chick from Houston while at Wooster. She used to cruise around in her Range Rover. She was a member of the Alpha Gamma Sorority. I vividly remember volunteering for a senior psychology experiment. She was there too, and it was raining outside. Walking her home under my golf umbrella sprung to my mind, but I did not follow through and ask. I also used to see her on campus and in the commons. Often she would smile in my direction. I even screwed up royally when her sorority sponsored a dance and I lacked the courage to ask her to be my partner. She got married to some incredibly lucky guy in 2003. There was one woman who outwardly liked me that first year. She was African-American and fairly lanky- a theater major. Some nights she would come to my room just to make out, but it never went any further. I do not know why I did not reach out to the opposite sex then. I wondered, was I young Ebenezer Scrooge in Charles Dickens' "A Christmas Carol?" A steady, healthy relationship could possibly have helped with stress brought on by the pressure I put on myself.

My second year at Wooster was marked by a serious depression stemming from my desire to transfer to a different college. I was looking at Williams College in northwestern Massachusetts, Ripon College in Wisconsin, and the honors program at the University of Wisconsin-Madison. With a 3.75 grade point average Williams still turned me down. Having attended Williams, my father was very upset. Ripon and Wisconsin both accepted me, but I decided to tough it out and complete my second year at Wooster. I had a very supportive roommate who was willing to back me up if that terrible first room-mate ever gave me any trouble. We went to meals together religiously along with golfers and had a good, healthy relationship except when it came time for Halloween. Lying on our dorm room floor was a fake dead person. At the time I was immersed in my political science major and was looking forward to a semester in Washington DC where I would be groomed for a career in government.

Leading up to 1992 National Elections and Aftermath up until American University

TO SAY THAT I was involved in politics from late 1991, especially the summer of 1992, up until the November 1992 elections is a bit of an understatement. From the fall of 1991 up until the elections I kept a scrapbook of the presidential race. In the spring of 1992 I went to Marquette University with my WWII veteran grandpa and my child-hood friend/enemy/competitor Andy to see presidential candidate Edmund Gerry Brown speak at a rally. Man, that guy could scream! His theme was "Take Back America." Bill Clinton had been gaining ground in the polls, so Brown knew that he had to get his message across. He almost won the WI Primary. Then beginning in late May I started volunteering for Marc Marotta for Congress. This was the guy that, at my age of twenty, lured me into the politics game.

Marotta was a securities attorney with the same law firm that my father represented- a nationwide encompassing firm with 250 lawyers just in Milwaukee alone. He worked for one of the top 15 or maybe even top 10 largest law firms in the US. The district Marc was running for had a strong Democrat following. Everyone knew a Democrat would win the general election in November. It was the September Democratic primary election winner that would be the eventual new member of Congress. Marc claimed to be a more conservative-leaning Democrat especially when it came to finance. He ran against a traditional Democrat and career state politician in Tom Barrett as well as Terrance Pitts- an inner city owner of funeral parlors.

Marotta sent me and another college-aged man whose father was also a lawyer with the same law firm to spy on Tom Barrett's announcement of candidacy party. Man was I being thrown to the wolves. The more liberal Barrett, the current Mayor of Milwaukee, eventually won but by attending his announcement I believe in this instance that I may have been framed and later would serve as the scapegoat upon later attending American University when Barrett was a Congressman. Try to follow how my childhood friend/enemy/teammate/competitor is linked to my downfall. Again, maybe a legitimate accusation but this was denied by psychiatrists and cognitive psychologists.

I went back to Wooster later that summer and on the night of Marc's primary I went for a run during thunderstorms in pouring rain. One of my golf teammates thought I was crazy. My folks gave me the bad news the next day that Marotta had finished 2nd in the primary with 31% of the vote- a very close 2nd. That same year, when home from college during the spring, I drove around Shorewood putting up campaign signs for my dad's bid for village trustee. He would serve in municipal government for the next 12 years with 6 as village president.

I remember vividly how Andy visited Marotta's campaign office during the summer. He shook Marc's huge hand(he was a college power forward on Marquette's basketball team back in the day), read his policy position papers, and then concluded and eventually told me that he and his father would be voting for Tom Barrett. Barrett also had a law degree and, to this very day, Andy is a lawyer in Washington DC as well as an author. Later that summer in mid August Andy and I met up at his house and went walking together on Lake Drive. We talked about topics such as how hard I had worked to get to this point in life. We argued, and then finally he said I was acting a bit pompous. I felt then and there like leveling him like I did back in 6th grade when after his team scored a touchdown in nerf football he came up to me and said," Ooh suck my hiny." I know that he never forgot this and never came to terms with it because I kicked his ass bad that day. I guess it is still vivid in my memory too. Anyway, his dad was dean of the nearby university and he, I believe, may have played a role in my breakdown 1 ½ weeks later in DC. All it would have taken was a phone call because Andy threatened me. He had been expressing, though maybe not directly, that his dad's position of power could influence my future. This gets into what I call the competition of disciplines that personally affected me throughout my medical care from 1993 to the present. Those who practice law, medicine, work in the insurance field, and serve in an academic realm etc. vie for power. In 2004 Andy's father even called, to my face, the Chief Financial Officer of my father's law firm by the last name Greedy when it is actually Grebe. I knew his last name and did not feel like stooping to his level and argue. His wife was right there when he said this. This sure sounds like jealousy to me and for what? Doesn't the dean of a large university make enough money? Or was he interested in revolutionizing the competition of disciplines by arguing on behalf of academia? Now and into the future I could never trust Andy nor his dad. To them, everything is political. There is little if any humanistic element. With politics there are winners and losers. No doubt they see me as the latter.

The American University

DURING THE LATE summer of 1993, at the age of 20, I embarked on a semester of government studies at American University in DC. There I would learn the ropes and ins and outs of our nation's capital. Most importantly, I would develop some political savvy and explore career paths. I had flown to New York first to be with relatives, and my demise was already beginning. I was upset because my computer was double and triple-checked for being hazardous at Milwaukee's airport. In New York I had trouble sleeping due to racing thoughts. During the days there I had been playing golf at Bethpage Park's Black Course- site of the 2002 and 2009 US Open. My dad and I played with a national security agent one afternoon. He was probably around 30 years old. After the round I asked him how many clients he has amassed in his short career. He responded by saying, "I just gained two today," which troubled me. All of this with the sleep deprivation and computer problems at Mitchell Airport sure had my mind spinning. One of my peer editors clarified with me that CIA or FBI agents do not have clients rather more like a list of people they keep track of.

Having driven for five or so hours we arrived at American University that hot August morning. I had been up since 4 AM and never do sleep well in cars. I remember asking a US Marine where room 0410 was located. He responded, "On the fourth floor," like I was some dummy. My roommate had driven up from Oklahoma and took some time sightseeing on his way up to DC. He went to an automobile race in Virginia and showed me his pictures of cars crashing and burning. Little did I know that I was literally going to crash and burn in DC. I remember jokingly telling my roommate that I wanted to get rich fast and retire at forty-five years old. On the very first night,(and my only night there)I chose to stay in and continue reading "The Great Gatsby," but for some strange reason my lights were flickering making it difficult to read. Consequently, I decided to go for a walk. I met a pretty blonde-haired woman outside of my building on the stoop. She was from Rollins College in Florida, and we talked about the pressures that parents place on their kids. She told me that her parents had a bunch of money in Swiss bank accounts. We maybe talked for a half hour. Then I decided to go to bed. It had been a long overwhelming week and day. In the middle of the night I remember grabbing some change and crawling to the pay phone to call my folks at their Georgetown hotel. The pay phone was jammed and would not accept any coins. I only panicked even more. The day before I had remembered my roommate telling me that he wanted to do his internship with Senator Bob Dole's office. I respect Dole for what he has done in retirement with his actions of pushing for the reintegration into the workforce of people with all types of disabilities.

On day two at American University I woke up to a pink sunrise. Yet another blazingly hot day ahead of me- could I take the heat? I showered and remembered not having a bathrobe, so I was walking down the hall to my room with solely a towel around my waist while young women giggled. Then I went to breakfast where I was joined by a couple of guys- one from Port Washington, WI and another from Madison, WI. I just did not feel all right. After breakfast all of us gathered in a nearby Episcopalian church to hear a speech by the dean of the Washington Semester Program.

The dean's speech did not make much sense and frightened me. He brought up things that truly made me question whether something was up with my computer check at General Mitchell Field in Milwaukee and the national security agent at Bethpage Black Golf Course on Long Island, New York. Next the dean talked about some hotshot 46-year-old lawyer being convicted of illegal insider trading. My father at that time was a 45 ½ year old corporate finance attorney. It made me wonder if my room or computer had been bugged since I had told my roommate that I wanted to get rich fast and retire young.

Before continuing, I would like to discuss the term "insider trading" and make it more easily understood by my readers. As defined in Wikipedia, "insider trading" is the buying and selling of a public company's stock or other securities by individuals with access to non-public information about the company. Some kinds of trading based on insider information are illegal. This is because it is seen as unfair to other investors who do not have access to the information, as the investor with insider information could potentially make larger profits than a typical investor could make. It may occur before mergers and/or acquisitions of companies are made public. Like a business transaction, everyday hundreds or even thousands of companies merge or are acquired. Let's suppose the chief financial officer or CFO of a publicly traded company owns 1,000 shares of the company stock where he/she works. Because he/she keeps the company's books, he/she notices a significant decline in the sales results and therefore knows that the company's profits will be tumbling. Before the decline in sales and profits are reported to the public, he/she sells all of his shares knowing that the price of the stock will fall when the news of the declining sales and profits becomes public. He/she has "traded" namely sold his/her shares on the basis of information known to him/her in that capacity and not known to the public.

Members of Congress through their cronyism and business ties back home have been known to pad their pockets by empowering themselves in this process of insider trading. It occurs with both money-hungry Democrats and Republicans, leftists, centrists, Tea Party and right wing members of Congress. Let's face it. Money and the ability to raise money breeds incumbency. Therefore, you will see some senators or representatives who have been in Congress for twenty even forty years. Term limit legislation has been sort of a joke for members of Congress. Senator John McCain(R-AZ)and former Senator Russ Feingold(D-WI)proposed term limits in the late 20th Century. Interestingly, McCain remains in Congress as of today while in his 80's. Feingold lost his Senate seat a few years back but soon had run to re-enter the Senate. He lost. I guess this is why they call politics a game as in Hedrick Smith's "The Power Game."

Let's continue with the dean's speech. Carrying on, the dean said "We in Washington" have the capability or power to make airplanes explode killing everyone aboard. My personal internship interest lay in national park reform legislation. I still remember the dean saying it was wisest to intern in more profitable areas like finance rather than something like environmental policy. He also alluded to the notion that some states were more important than others, and I felt my allegiance to Wisconsin and Ohio burn inside of me. Earlier that same morning before breakfast I held up a quarter to my eyes and said separation of state. I have always believed that there should be choice when parents decide which schools are best for their kids whether they be public, private, parochial, technology driven ones, or special education ones etc. The dean, at the very end of his speech, said, "Oh yeah and separation of church and state? That is the way it will always be." I felt a lump in my throat. Now do you think my room had been bugged? Finally, the dean had said something like, "You'll get another chance."

It was a time for desperate measures after the dean's speech. I raced to the campus police station and told the officers that I needed to see my parents. My parents arrived some two hours later, and it was only a matter of minutes before I withdrew from American University's Washington Semester Program. We did not pack up my things and leave without a conference, and I even remember my dad arguing with university personnel about a 1982 airplane crash in which almost everyone died when it faltered, hit a bridge, and ended up in the Potomac River. There were prominent business professionals on that plane, and he knew some of them. My dad believed that the incoming class had been subjected to psychological manipulation by the dean. I have no doubts to this day that the dean was taking the form of the Devil. Unfortunately, I would cross paths in Milwaukee with a similar individual in the future.

Leaving out the airplane crash that my dad had referred to would be a mistake and deserves some attention. In 1982 an Air Florida Boeing 737 crashed in Washington DC on a cold January day. Weather was the cause, but it certainly could have been prevented. It was 4 PM in DC and the doomed flight had already been waiting for an hour after preventative maintenance while the wings were accumulating more and more ice. Blame went to the captain for making a poor decision to takeoff, but personnel at the airport had helped in the decision making. After all, there was only one runway open at the time. The flight was headed to Fort Lauderdale with a brief stop in Tampa, but it never got more than a few hundred feet off of the ground as ice had added weight to the wings. The plane ended up in the icy Potomac River after crashing onto a road bridge. Six passengers survived the crash of the eighty onboard, and one of these died drowning. Two years later Air Florida went bankrupt like many 1980's airlines.

I remember flying into and out of Nashville, TN back in 2002. I was visiting a former history professor assistant from the same university that Andy's dad had worked at. Andy's father had been part of the history faculty. Flying to Nashville was a major pain in the ass. First, I had to fly to Chicago O'Hare with a layover of more than 2 hours. Next, I flew to Nashville on a United Express Airbus and arrived very late. We still had a one hour drive from the airport to where my friend lived in McMinnville. The flight back to Milwaukee was a stark contrast. I was supposed to just retrace my tracks by flying United to Chicago and then on to Milwaukee, but airline personnel told me to follow them out onto the tarmac to an airplane that was waiting for passengers to board. This was a Midwest Express Airlines smaller jet that had a capacity of maybe 40 passengers. Anyway, I climbed the stairs onto the plane and two very young men with crew cuts greeted me. I did not ask them, but they must have been fresh out of the Air Force. The flight was very pleasant. The captain and co-captain flew at lower altitudes than I had never experienced before and were pointing out landmarks along the way. I felt very safe. I guess I'll never know why I was blessed with these circumstances, however, as my story progresses you might be able to draw conclusions.

American University Aftermath

UPON LEAVING THE American University's Tenley Campus we headed for my parents' hotel room. My dad went across the street to purchase some dinner. I vividly remember him returning with some deli sandwiches and three Snapple drinks. The first thing that came to my manic mind was that the beverages were poisoned. I had already been a nervous wreck walking from our parking spot to the hotel earlier. My parents were very concerned about my paranoia, and this prompted them to call an ambulance to take me to Georgetown University Hospital. The paramedic entered our hotel room carrying a toy machine gun with a red light that flickered upon pulling the trigger. I thought this guy was strange. I am sure the feelings were mutual. Gosh was I even more paranoid at this point. I spent five and one half days in the hospital. My doctor concluded that I should take a semester or two off from my studies, psychologically regroup, and then plan to return to college.

The plan was to fly from New York back to Milwaukee. After what the dean had said about airplanes exploding or crashing, I was very nervous on that flight back home. It was refreshing to be back in Milwaukee. My parents were referred to a psychiatrist through a family friend. I thought that I was supposed to be resting up with hopes of returning to college. Instead, my doctor at Milwaukee Psychiatric Hospital prescribed six psychotropic medications including among others Haldol, Ativan, Cogentyne, and Lithium Carbonate. These medications were so powerful in affecting my concentration that I could only read nine pages of Alex Haley's book "Roots." My manic episode in Washington DC was followed by a time of intense depression. It is extremely difficult to concentrate much less read when depressed. The desire is not there. All I wanted to do was sleep due to the medications. Motivation to do just about anything like exercising is hard to come by.

My psychiatrist was not the most professional in his field and at Milwaukee Psychiatric Hospital. He possessed some habits and methods that disturbed me greatly causing me to hate him and desire another doctor. For example, he was a chain smoker and almost always fired up a grit just before my sessions. About the most disturbing aspect of his style was his repeatedly asking me if I had thoughts of suicide. Mention of suicide contributed to my frailty. Also, he ordered blood draws once or twice per week due to the need to find a therapeutic range of the Lithium in my system. That was professional and, over the course of twenty-four plus years, I have been stuck with needles close to 500 times. I have scar tissue, and it is difficult for the phlebotomist to find healthy veins to access. I began seeing this particular doctor in September of 1993, but he had a heart attack in April after I halted communication with him.

I remember how manic I was during the summer of 1994. Evenings were marked by long runs north to the Fox Point border and back. What followed included two things: driving my running route so as to clock the mileage and devouring a sugary Hostess fruit pie simultaneously. I became very thin that summer because the mania had given me a surge in energy. The reason for the manic episodes was my quitting all of my medications shortly after my shrink suffered his April heart attack. I was as light as a feather but still in good physical shape from all of the running, swimming, and even some weightlifting. How could I possibly be ready for another semester at the College of Wooster?

The College of Wooster Revisited

TRAVELING TO WOOSTER was memorable. My folks had recently bought me a used Mazda Protégé for this late August 1994 trip. I made good time with only having to stop once to take a leak behind a dumpster. What can I say? There were no bathrooms around, and I simply could not wait. This may have been a serious lack of judgment on my part due to mania. I had chosen to take US 30 for my route after passing through Chicago and then on to beautiful Fort Wayne, Indiana. Highway US 30 has far less semi-trucks than the Ohio Turnpike, but the speed limit is only 55 mph.

It felt good to be back in Wooster. I would be living in an off-campus house with three other guys. I arrived to find an empty house, so I began unpacking my belongings including cases of good old Wisconsin beer. Exercising that summer decreased my weight to 160 pounds. That is not very much for a guy standing just under six feet tall. Some of my housemates arrived shortly, and we headed for the better of the two grocery stores. I am always looking for good deals but got out of hand- a symptom of bipolar disorder I suppose. Upon arriving back home we filled up the pantry and refrigerator with mostly stuff that I had selected: soda, ground chuck for burgers and tacos, rib-eye steak, frozen veggies, cottage cheese, ice cream, bread, and some chips among other things. In addition, there were all of the condiments to flavor the food. It was a shame that I barely made a dent in any of this. The reason for this was, after about one week, I experienced a serious episode of hypomania.

I had no idea that I was going to "hit the wall" after less than one week upon returning to Wooster. I was simply so driven to put my feelings and thoughts down in writing regarding my experience at American University the year before. Shortly after dinnertime until early morning I reeled off 19 ½ pages, but I did not stop there. I called a close lady friend from the Fox Valley in WI whom I will refer to as "Country Girl." I called to warn her to be careful and safe in her daily routine because I thought that people who had affected me were also in danger. Not stopping there, I called the attorney who ran for Congress back in 1992. I pissed off his wife because the phone call was back to Milwaukee to the central time zone, and it was before 7 AM there. Not only was I manic. There was definitely some paranoia creeping into my mind. You know what they say about paranoia? It will destroy ya. My major regret about having to call my parents to come and pick me up was a new relationship I had started with a woman whose last name was Morse and she was from Ithaca, New York where I was born.

I stapled my lengthy essay and headed for the dean of students' office. I can't recall if I ever made it there, but let's just say there might have been good reason to believe I had since the dean died recently at age sixty-seven. He was never close to the student body and ran the school like a businessman instead of a humanist. My closest housemate, my first semester friend jogging partner, knew that I must have had some type of chemical imbalance in my brain that needed to be treated with medication. I had not taken any since early April of that year.

From what I remember, my friend ran after me and convinced me to visit Hygeia Health Center. To this day I still cannot find that extensive story that I wrote while pulling that all-nighter. I was well taken care of at the health center, and my parents were notified. They planned to drive to Wooster the next day. I remember the health center staff allowing me to have cranberry/grape juice- one of my favorites. My freshman and sophomore year geology professor came to visit me. During the summer he used to lead alumni and family on whitewater rafting trips down the Colorado River. As he left he said,"Best wishes in all of your endeavors." This meant a lot to me coming from my favorite professor at the College of Wooster. I consider the undertaking of writing this book to be an endeavor. I would never see Wooster again. I still have a big place in my heart for the excellent faculty that I experienced there. Even though I only studied at Wooster for two years, they still consider me alumni of the class of 1996. Now it was time for me to reconnect with new medical professionals.

Ripon College

I TRANSFERRED TO Ripon College in August of 1995 at the age of 22. My favorite PGA Tour golfer won the Greater Milwaukee Open my first weekend at Ripon. I made an effort to run cross-country, so my physical health was good. I was so lucky at the GMO for having met my favorite player and his immediate family the day before his victory. They gave me a pass for Sunday's final round. Graciously, his wife invited me into the small circle of family and friends on the 18th green after the victory was official. The rest is history. We have dined together and still keep in touch. He won again in Milwaukee in 1997 by sinking an eagle chip on the last hole. It was then that I hooked up with his caddie. He was from Jacksonville, FL and we went to a Milwaukee Brewer game one night the week of the golf tournament. In the past he had carried the golf bag for the winners of three major championships. He sadly died from a brain tumor after the turn of the century. My family has been lucky. My favorite player has given us free passes to major championships like the US Open and PGA Championship.

While studying at Ripon I had a love affair with Lane Library. This, however, was not that unhealthy of a relationship like at Wooster. I was on the golf team playing #2 man, played intramural basketball and flag football, and I even had a few girlfriends. Still, my studies always came first and I had very demanding professors so much so that I even took ¾ the course load for two semesters while there. My adviser and professor for two classes was a Scottish man. He saw right through my common everyday mood swings and used to often put his index fingers at the corner of his lips and tell me to smile.

Ripon was a quaint little city with a lot of history. Boasting as being the founding location of the Republican Party, Ripon did not seem all that conservative. Faculty members were mostly independent, and there was a good mix amongst the students both politically and socially. I remember my first semester well because it was the first time in 2 ½ years that I had been a full-time college student. Carrying a semester load of 16 credits was a mistake. I felt I had to drop an interesting and demanding course called "The Rhetoric of Social Movements." My favorite course was a tie between "US Foreign Policy" and "Early America: Settlement to Revolution." While at Ripon I never had a roommate. I made friends, but I never had to directly share my mental illness with anyone. In fact, I never told any of my Ripon friends except one as of recent about my mental illness. This was 1995-1997, and I was only on Lithium Carbonate. I always felt I needed some type of antidepressant, but studies show that these medications do very little for bipolar disorder. The evolution of antipsychotics would change this. I currently have one in my repertoire. When taking meds I always fought depression and rarely mania.

Studying in Chicago with the Associated Colleges of the Midwest's Urban Studies Program and my May of 1997 graduation with honors marked my two greatest memories/achievements while a student representing Ripon. Chicago is a fascinating place to live and work. I had four housemates in our flat apartment in the Logan Square Neighborhood- primarily a Mexican and Puerto Rican section northwest of the city. One of my housemates was Vietnamese, two were Latino, and the fourth was Caucasian with some Native American blood. They were from Iowa, Colorado, Minnesota, and Illinois. Having housemates was a big adjustment for me compared to my space and freedom at Ripon. Sometimes I did not handle things so well like when my female Latino housemate left her used maxi-pads in the pantry where we kept some of our food. I went on a tirade.

Interning in Chicago impacted me so much that I developed my thesis while there. I worked for the Lake Michigan Federation- now the Alliance for the Great Lakes. My major assignment was to research and write a paper on non-point source pollution from tributaries into Lake Michigan and to research the number of storm water outfalls to Lake Michigan in the city limits. Astonishingly through interviews and hard-nosed library research, I came up with a number of outfalls that was far greater than the ancient data.

My Lake Michigan Federation research led to the infancy of my senior thesis on Chicago and Milwaukee's Deep Tunnel Project for the management of wastewater and storm water. I wrote an extensive thesis on this subject and really delved into public works history in the Midwest. All of the urban studies program students purchased monthly passes good for the buses and, more importantly, the elevated train and subway system(The EL). I was busy utilizing the EL throughout the entire city visiting places like the Department of Sewers, the United States Environmental Protection Agency #5, and the Metropolitan Water Reclamation District of Greater Chicago(MWRDGC). I was able to interview some specialists, and all of the people in the public information bureaus for the agencies were extremely helpful. It is a bit of an understatement as to how much pavement I pounded in those three months.

The other fond memory was graduation in May of 1997. I graduated cum laude(3.57 grade point average)with honors in pogo or politics and government. Fortunately, my WWII veteran grandfather was there for the ceremony as were my parents, sister, and brother-in-law.

I also studied under a very interesting psychology professor while at Ripon. He was my professor for only one class: "Theories of Personality." We have developed a good relationship over the years and remain quality friends to this very day. We play golf together in Green Lake and Fond du Lac, WI. After a round, we usually get lunch or dinner and just engage in good conversation. My wife has met this friend of mine on a few occasions.

My favorite experience with my professor friend occurred when we paddled his canoe down the White River near Princeton, WI and fished for smallmouth bass. This brought back fond memories of my childhood and early adult life having canoed the lake where my parents' seasonal home is located as well as the lakes and rivers of the

Boundary Waters on the Minnesota/Canadian border. This professor friend has always been there for good advice. When I was attending psychiatric sessions only once every month or two it was nice to have him readily respond to my emails. Today we communicate via email, facebook, and on the phone every week to two weeks.

University of
Wisconsin-Milwaukee

DURING THE SUMMER of 1993 before heading to American University I took a cultural anthropology course at UW-Milwaukee. It was difficult taking this intensive, 4-week course while working at the Department of Public Works. My journal for the class saved my ass in that it allowed me to get a "B" grade when my test scores were lower. I met a beautiful woman in this class and went out on a date with her. After eating at a trendy restaurant I was embarrassed because I had forgotten my wallet. She paid, and we decided to take a walk on the trails leading to Lake Michigan. I took her to the woods on private property where the mosquitoes were terrible. When I told her a mosquito had bitten me, her reply was, "I bet you taste good." I wish I could say and the rest was history, but we did not go any further than making out in her car in my driveway. We did discuss the importance of reciprocity when it came to giving and receiving oral sex in a healthy relationship. One more date with this woman, and we probably would have engaged in some good, intense sex. People with bipolar disorder, although not diagnosed at this time, are often sexually promiscuous. Here it might be just two young and horny adults, but there is a noticeable pattern throughout my memoir.

I am sure that my mania had started that summer due to my excessive contributions in classroom discussion. This also included a louder than normal tone as well as a "hogging" of the topic at hand. Needless to say, my anthropology professor told me not to forget about her when I get to the top in life.

During the spring of 1995 I took two political science courses. One was called "State and Local Politics" while the other was called "Public Administration." I had to devote a large amount of time to these courses because they required much memorization. There were not any papers like at Wooster and Ripon. I still managed to get "A's" in both. For this semester I stopped in at the university's Student Accessibility Center and talked to its director. He was a blind man who had me sit down and told me that I could still be successful in college. I was not afraid to ask for special accommodations in my two classes. Upon request I was allowed to take exams in a different room than the rest of the students. In addition, I was given extra time. That late spring I turned in all of my necessary documents to Ripon College. I was ready to transfer in August of 1995. Colleges like Ripon and Wooster emphasize producing more well-rounded students in terms of both speaking and writing ability. You have to write more papers at these schools and there is a greater requirement to participate in classroom discussion. I would attend UW-Milwaukee yet again starting in 1998 for a social studies teacher training program.

After graduating from Ripon in 1997 I took one year off and worked at Lincoln Park Golf Course on the grounds crew. I worked there from the summer of 1996 to the summer of 2001. Fortunately, in 1997 I worked enough hours to be eligible for unemployment compensation during winter layoffs. The money that I made collecting unemployment for the winter of 1997-98 paid for 3/4 of the purchase of my 1998 used fishing boat. I no longer have the boat because my parents sold it this past summer. It was my pride and joy. Cooper, my springer spaniel from 1999-2015, loved it too. We traveled all over northern WI in my family's fishing van towing my boat. In the spring of 1998 I returned to Lincoln and enrolled at UW-Milwaukee for the post baccalaureate social studies teacher program. The summer of 1998 consisted of early 4 and 5 AM shifts at the golf course followed by two afternoon classes. I was the only guy in one of them but still was not able to get a date. In one class I earned an "A" while the other a "B-." I was on my way to becoming a teacher.

The fall semester of 1998 represented a time of readjustment to school life for me. I had to enroll in some prerequisite courses, so I took "Western Civilization 1500-present." The professor was a great lecturer, and the teacher's assistant was second to none. I had a crush on her, but nothing except a short-term friendship fulfilled that desire. We frequented Mexican restaurants on occasion with other couples. She was British, and I absolutely loved her accent. I did grow a beard that semester and looked like a true freak of nature. I was obsessed with my teacher's assistant all the way up until the time I found out she was dating. Another student beat me to her. I still befriended them both and invited them to my family's seasonal home on Lake Ellen in southern Sheboygan County. Anyway, I earned an "A" in the course and wrote a fantastic essay comparing and contrasting fascism with communism.

The following spring semester I enrolled in "US History: Civil War Reconstruction to the present." Again, I had a British teacher's assistant only this time it was a guy. I earned an "A" in this course also. We also frequently went out for Mexican food the summer after the course. He worked a day job in the Latino neighborhoods and took the bus. I would often pick him up and we would dine at Tres Hermanos on Lincoln Ave. and La Taqueria Esmeralda on Greenfield Ave. I would later visit him in Tennessee on two different occasions in 2002 alone and in 2004 with my father. A trustworthy friend, I asked him to be my campaign manager if I ever desired to run for Congress. His response was that he would love to, but he was planning on going home to England to marry his sweetheart and embark on a career in real estate. That was the last time I ever heard from him. Oh, how I wish he could be part of my life spending quality time with me in a supportive role that he had maintained up until the time of his departure. This makes me think of Elton John's lyrics, "Daniel is traveling tonight on a plane. I can see the red-tailed lights....." Up until that time in my life he was the closest thing to a brother that I never had.

In 1999 and 2000 I enrolled in courses that were more geared towards educating middle and high school-aged students. My student teaching went very well in the fall of 1999. I was assigned to a middle school near the Milwaukee County Courthouse to aid in teaching 8th grade US History. This was a school geared towards the health sciences and was also across the street from a hospital. It was also located in the same neighborhood as halfway houses. Students had tough lives, and their guardians(grandparent, uncle, aunt and mother and/or father)worked hard without having the time or skills to help the students with their homework. Consequently, there was not much homework but there were quizzes, some tests, and quasi book reports. I was student teaching with another UW-Milwaukee student, and we decided along with our cooperating teacher that we would maximize the time spent in the classroom. My responsibility was the 2nd hour class. I whipped them into shape by teaching them about colonial America, the Constitution, and geography with the incorporation of music. For example, I would play jazz music when they were learning about cities and states like New Orleans, Louisiana and St. Louis, Missouri. I played "Dueling Banjos" to help them learn that Georgia was very rural. For a history lesson of 1945-1990 I played Billy Joel's "We didn't start the fire" and asked the kids to research at least three lines from the song. When it came time for the students to research a career I remember helping a kid that wanted to be a firefighter. I told him that my uncle was a firefighter in New York, and I also gave a lesson on Ben Franklin stating that among other things Franklin believed society must have fire departments. It was a memorable semester, and I still have pictures that I took of all of my 8th graders. As much as I cheered the students on with their studies, they supported me with my October Milwaukee Lakefront Marathon. I brought my 5 sports medals and told the kids they would achieve great things in life as they mature. I even helped some of them get summer employment caddying at nearby golf courses.

The following winter and spring semester of 2000 I student taught at one of the toughest Milwaukee Public high schools. I remember being anxious and wanting to get my hands on the textbooks before the semester began. My cooperating teacher never returned my calls, but this was for the best. He made me comfortable and helped me ease into the semester by teaching the first two weeks. Some people call it SAD or seasonal affective disorder. I was having a difficult time adjusting to my role. My lesson planning took excessive amounts of time. I decided to start decreasing one of my medications- a big mistake.

My students were great. I only had nineteen and ten students in my 9th and 10th hour Law and Government classes. I also taught remedial US History, but my cooperating teacher simply told me to give the students seatwork worksheets for every book chapter. To check on out of class reading for Law and Government, I would assign in-class 5'ers and 10'ers- a teaching method used by my cooperating teacher. They were five and ten-line responses to a major question or key theme from their reading. My greatest strength was assessment. Quizzes and exams would always match the content that was covered so that students would not feel clueless or aimless in their preparation. We had fun in class studying the Bill of Rights. I think that the students enjoyed studying the death penalty and criminal law the most. On a personal note, the students in both classes supported me when I got back into running and was losing weight. Why did I have the energy to start running again after a winter of cookies and chocolates and brutal weather? The reduction in medication gave me this energy. Maybe my local university supervisor who would assess my teaching style on appointment caught on to my mood changes. Still, he stooped very low on my birthday and asked me if I really wanted to teach for a career. Throughout middle and high school student-teaching we had a seriously shaky relationship.

I taught a dynamite lesson on the US involvement in Vietnam in the remedial US History course. I broke down the Vietnam Conflict into all of the areas of the social studies even anthropology and sociology. I defined the disciplines within and gave two or three examples minimum. As 20% of their final exam the students had to apply the same model to the Persian Gulf Crisis and the war in Iraq and Afghanistan. The other 80% was completely remedial: two true or false questions per chapter open book. It drove them crazy and made me smile and chuckle.

What a dream come true I thought for being extended an interview where I did my 8th grade student teaching. The panel consisted of a parent that had called me, the principal, the librarian, and three teachers- all male. Fully decked out in my new suit, I think that I was overdressed for the interview. I was nervous too. They had a series of questions tucked under the glass table top in front of me. I told the panel that my teaching style enabled the kids to rise up and care for their studies during my student teaching. I told them that I planned to teach for 25-30 years and then make a spirited run for Congress. They all looked at me in amazement except the principal seemed like he was in disbelief. I was having a difficult time answering all of the questions, but it seemed like the librarian really wanted me to get the job. She asked questions fairly rapidly to increase my chances of completing them. I remember the principal leaving the room for a phone call twice, and he did tell me that there was another interview after mine. The parent on the panel knew one of the politicians that I had volunteered for back in 1994. In hindsight, the women on the panel were going to bat for me. The principal assured me that I would receive a follow up phone call in 7-10 days.

Instead of a 7-10 day response, the principal called on a mid July Saturday afternoon more than two months later. My folks were at a golf outing. At first the principal tried comforting me for not getting hired, but that was past news to me. I was sure the position had been filled. Maybe I sounded confrontational, and he shot back, "Oh, now don't get depressed." For the rest of the conversation he breathed heavily into the phone and said that he hated my family. To this day, I have a strong hunch that this principal must have done a thorough background check and found out about my mental illness. Maybe the link was that his son Nick was friends with one of my family friends. You know how much gossip there is in the suburbs. Later that summer I was hired by another K-12 Milwaukee Public School to teach social studies. This large school district holds a one week orientation. I crossed paths with that devilish principal there. He just had a big smile on his face. A couple of days later I checked into Milwaukee

Psychiatric Hospital. An English teacher from that principal's school also checked into the same hospital. He saw me there when he visited her. All I know is that her boss was on some kind of a power trip using his administrative position and contacts in hospitals to discover my diagnosis. His phone call had really messed me up all the way to the orientation. I simply could not function as an educator. I am still bothered by the fact this ever happened. Maybe I should have taken my mom's advice and studed journalism instead of teaching. My dead grandfather, who had been in Air Force Intelligence during WWII, inspired me to teach like he did after his military service. He would have been thrilled with my choice but rolling in his grave with what had happened to me.

Another interesting note is the fact that one day during student teaching at that principal's school we were having an assembly and the American flag was draped all over the floor of the stage that morning. How disrespectful! This was the same day that pro golfer Payne Stewart's Lear Jet climbed way too high to 50,000 feet and everyone on the plane died as it went into autopilot and finally crashed in South Dakota. I loved Stewart's gracefulness on the golf course, and very few sports professionals even came close to his model of sincere patriotism. Also, the principal invited leaders from the Senegal delegation to the middle school. They wore all kinds of gold jewelry. There must have been some kickbacks for the principal and possible shady financial matters.

Mental Hospitals Introduction

MENTAL HOSPITALS ARE really not all that different in daily structure than what I imagine a prison is like. In both cases most often, medications are administered. The environment is such that patients have to inquire at the grand main desk if they want or need anything. If not the main desk, then patients or inmates have to ask someone in authority. Although nurses distribute snacks, patients are able to keep their own personal snacks behind the main desk in a storage room. Blood is drawn first thing in the morning, laundry facilities exist, there are multiple TV rooms, and there is an outdoor, enclosed-in area for smoking. Other daily activities include arts and crafts, music therapy, and exercising in a gym facility.

One interesting thing to note at Milwaukee County Mental Health Complex the staff personnel of color treated me better. Remember, I was once told that my black Marine Corps boss from the golf course was the County. I wonder to this day if he had anything to do with my treatment. Finally, there was always cutthroat competition for coffee at meals, the chosen TV channel, the patient phone, and mid-day and evening snacks.

Georgetown University Hospital late August 1993

WHAT CAUSED ME to arrive at Georgetown University Hospital and what followed had been a nightmare. I remember one doctor at the hospital telling my dad that his profession was going to rot. The personnel at the hospital acted, for the most part, very professional but some of their conclusions did not make sense. A technician performed an MRI on my brain. Remembering that metal colander apparatus I wore still makes me feel like I was part of an experiment. The technician brushed water over this helmet-like thing, and the brush seemed like horse hair. I returned to my bedroom and fell asleep. In the middle of the night I was frightened by a scary African American man who visited me to draw blood. All I could see was his white eyeballs. The next day I was moved to a different bedroom with an eerie light above my head. I remember reading a "Golf Digest" there describing Lee Janzen's victory at the US Open earlier that summer. I was interrupted by a nurse at this time, and she told me that I was an introvert. This conclusion still seems pretty much false given the fact that I am always calling friends to organize social gatherings. On another occasion two heavy-set doctors came into my room and wanted to pull on my arms to see if I was all together or something. I remember thinking that these guys were going to break my arm. The medications gave me strong hunger urges and cravings, and I finished off a pan of good chocolate brownies in just a few days. I can still remember the first and last names of some of the professionals that took care of me and that I worked with at the hospital. Finally, I had one last meeting with psychiatrists, psychologists, a few nurses, and a social worker in which one of them said, "This will never happen again." I was so drugged that I only comprehended but could not process it at the time.

Milwaukee County/ Columbia Hospitals

ARRIVING AT MILWAUKEE County Hospital in September of 1994 was one of the most animated experiences in my life. I had just returned from my manic episode at the College of Wooster, but the mania did not subside. My parents obviously were very concerned, so they called my grandfather in New York and asked him to come to Milwaukee and visit me. He and I went to Ma Fischer's restaurant for breakfast one day, but I did not go empty-handed. I brought a duffel bag full of clothes and a football like I was about to join the Army. In addition, I wore my eagle feather in my headband.

I left my grandpa and my belongings at Ma Fischer's and went to some bar called Jakester's. I used to watch baseball there on occasion. I did not have my wallet and was carrying around rolled-up dollar bills. I drank a beer at the bar, but do notice that I rarely got out of hand with alcohol. Drunkenness is very common for people with mental illnesses. I decided to walk after having that beer, so I headed west. I got pretty far and then encountered a busy street. I wanted to cross, so I went out to the median and waited. I was near a police station, so not before long an officer pulled me aside and put on handcuffs. Suspicions at first were drugs and/or alcohol, but they would soon learn that what I needed was psychiatric drugs.

Milwaukee County Hospital was a real circus. I arrived there and personnel went over the rules with me right off the bat. Bodily fluids could not be exchanged on the premises. There was a young woman that use to float around in the halls and stick her head in my bedroom asking me how my libido or sex drive was at the time. Mania is often personified by a heightened sex drive. This woman was absolutely gorgeous: a short-haired brunette with narrow brown eyes. I was only at County for ten days, but I managed to make out with this woman on occasion thus violating the exchange of bodily fluids rule. We could have gone so much farther. I also kissed another female patient on the unit. You meet a bunch of interesting characters at a mental hospital. One patient wanted me to sell the drug "Ice" for him when I was released. Then there was this light-skinned black woman who grabbed and stroked my penis when I had a friend visiting. Only once before as a kid at summer camp had I been sexually molested, but this time it was fun due to my mania. Another male patient looked like and claimed to be the actor Tommy Lee Jones, and he was even religiously doing one-handed push-ups. On one occasion the staff at County strapped me to a gurney with thick leather belts. This place was a haven for containing the manic patients until sedating medications could take effect. Luckily, my stay this time at County was short as I was transferred to Columbia Hospital.

Columbia Hospital in the fall of 1994 proved to be a blessing for me because I was first officially diagnosed with having bipolar disorder. My roommate was a short black man with a beard. He and I used to do push-ups and sit-ups before going to bed. Yes, another example of mania kicking in, but at least this was in a healthy way. Once we got a pass to leave the hospital grounds. We ended up going to Open Pantry to drink pints of Miller Genuine Draft. Another time only I got a pass. My roommate asked me to get him a pack of cigarettes. He was released before me, and he did not leave without stealing something of mine. Previously on the far side of the room across from my bed was my Martin Luther King, Jr. calendar. It mysteriously disappeared. There were also two female patients that we would hang out with watching television and chatting. One of them, who later had an affair with me, snuck in bottles of Zima clear malt beverage. Still, I never resorted to any form of alcoholism.

The female patient that came on to me after our release was a professional and had been divorced. We had good times together, but she enjoyed her wine too much. In addition, she had suicidal tendencies. For example, she shattered part of a wine glass and used the sharp remains to cut herself near her wrists. This was the volatile part of our brief relationship because I did not know what to do having little experience in this area of mental health. Probably the best thing I could do for her was just to be there for comfort. I feared that she would have hated me if I had her readmitted. I have fond memories of the night she invited me to sleep over. We danced to the "Forrest Gump" soundtrack in her upper duplex and ate her homemade ground turkey chili. It felt very good being close to her all night long.

I finally found a new psychiatrist while at Columbia and for the next six years. He was a short Indian man who had a picture of Gandhi in his office. This doctor was considered a wizard with medications, and he soon had me headed in the right direction with my health. My fall of 1994 hospitalizations allowed me again to set goals, enter college life again and not reside in another hospital until the summer of 2000. During this six-year span I followed doctor's orders, but I truthfully did not take it upon myself to learn about my mental illness. Later on, I would depart from this medical genius doctor because he did not provide psychotherapy, and I did not care for his referrals in this regard.

There were two psychotherapists taking care of me for part of the time consecutively from 1994-1999. Both were recommended by my pastor. While I had been at odds with my pastor initially, this advice helped me keep it together enough of the time to stay stable during those six years. The first was a big man like the Ghost of Christmas Present in Dickens' "A Christmas Carol." He would later move to central Illinois. Like most psychotherapists I think, both professionals had relaxing tea bags in their waiting rooms along with a pot of hot water. I took advantage. The second guy was more hip and not as traditional. He rode a BMW motorcycle and specialized in hypnotism. I remember selling him my moms' irons golf set for his daughter. When he moved offices from Whitefish Bay near church to the 3rd Ward he got a little creepy. Soon he would move to California.

Milwaukee Psychiatric Hospital Summer 2000

ONE MAJOR DIFFERENCE with this hospitalization in contrast to all of my others was the fact that I checked into the facility all by myself. My reasons stemmed from the overwhelming stress related to finding an entry level social studies teaching job. I arrived at the hospital in the evening both mentally and physically exhausted. My nurse was a no-nonsense Eastern European woman who asked if I wanted any food or drink. My request for pineapple-orange juice was honored along with a generous portion of macaroni and cheese. Early the next morning I had a seizure, and I almost fell into the shower stall. The side effects of stress and medication were the cause.

Milwaukee Psychiatric Hospital was a competitive environment. Patients were always kissing up to the staff in search of favoritism. One annoying routine involved patients walking briskly in the hall-way covering the perimeter of the unit. In addition, patients would display their competitiveness for use of the washers and dryers. It felt to me like witchcraft was occurring. For example, during relapse prevention group, other members would point their pencils at me and I felt a burning sensation in my loins. Vital signs were checked daily. It seemed that whenever my heartbeat was listened to there would be a thump and sharp pain in my chest. One night I decided to climb into my portable closet and close the door. It was almost as if I was in "The Lion, The Witch and The Wardrobe" as I felt my soul being ripped from my chest. When we behaved ourselves, they would let us go out on the patio for fresh air. Outside it seemed that the blood in my head would curdle as they had this large generator making tons of noise. Maybe it was the air conditioner. I don't know. Also, some of the nurses were very horny. I remember one of them gyrating her hips and shaking her ass when she left my room.

Four people had a lasting impact on me during this stay at Milwaukee Psychiatric Hospital. I still had my Indian doctor seeing me there regularly. It was up to him when I was to be released. He was not always around though, so I saw one backup psychiatrist in particular who I believed to be Satan. He interviewed me thoroughly and then met with my parents and I. His eyes glowed a vibrant orange as he told my mom and dad that we had a good talk. I felt like he wanted me to serve as his little drummer boy.

On the flip side, I was blessed with one great nurse for second shift. She used to take the time to read "Fishcamp" to me as I was getting ready for bed. Only one of my Columbia Hospital nurses rivaled her in the treatment given me. She was definitely an angel!

Later on during my hospital stay there arrived a pretty blonde-haired, blue-eyed patient claiming she was from Brazil. I was the only young male on the unit, so she naturally felt inclined to hang out with me. It got so intense that one late morning she came into my bedroom, took a flying leap towards me in bed, and told me that there was not much time and that we had to make love. Unfortunately, one of the nurses saw her go into my bedroom. We did not get very far, and all of the medications hindered me from actually being in the mood. I was like a zombie.

Milwaukee County Hospital Summer 2001

DURING THE LATE winter of 2000-01 I reduced my Lithium Carbonate dosage without notifying any doctors. In early April my dad and I went on a road trip to play some golf in Tennessee and Alabama. We drove straight through to McMinnville, TN where my former British teacher's assistant lived and worked in historic preservation. Medication withdrawal was a bit painful. It usually involved feelings of tiredness and long-lasting, throbbing headaches. I still managed to have a good time playing Fall Creek Falls State Park Golf Course. After our round of golf we ate lunch, went back to my friend's apartment, and drank MGD bottles while watching the Masters golf tournament. My friend was grateful that my dad picked up the tab for so many of our activities during our stay in TN. I was too.

Early the next morning my dad and I drove to Scottsboro, AL to play 36 holes of golf. My dad got a hole-in-one on our 31st hole- a picturesque 190-yard par 3 over the Tennessee River. He has done this five times in his golfing career, but this was at the beginning of the season whereas the others were all in the summer or early fall. I took a picture of the hole, framed it and gave it to my dad for Father's Day. Driving back to Wisconsin was no fun. Who would want to leave weather in the 70's to return to WI? I felt depressed so much so that I did not even want to stay an extra night so that the following day we could hike Kentucky's Mammoth Cave. It was only a matter of time before I would need to visit the hospital again. The medication reduction had caught up to me.

The circumstances of my arrival at County Hospital starkly contrasted to my visit to Milwaukee Psychiatric Hospital. Again, I had reduced my Lithium Carbonate. I worked that day at Lincoln Park

Golf Course as part of the golf course maintenance crew. The previous night I even cut grass with lights in the dark. My boss was a US Marine Corps veteran from the Vietnam era, and he expected us to be excited and thrilled to work this gung-ho job. We had mutual respect. I sometimes worked alone, and he entrusted the golf course property to me a few nights during the week. I punched out at 11 PM that Sunday night and arrived home only to get in a serious argument with my parents. One parent called the police, and they brought me to the hospital wearing handcuffs early the next morning. I remember hallucinating about my golf ball collection. One ball had the US Secret Service logo on it while the other was a 90 compression Titleist #6 balata ball given to me by my favorite golfer. I thought these were magic golf balls. Anyway, the local cops put the cuffs on tight. They raced me to the hospital on County grounds. Next, they left me in the squad car in that sweltering mid July heat for five or ten minutes. I could barely breathe as there was no air conditioner on at the time. Finally, they opened my door and took off the cuffs surrendering me to County medical personnel.

I entered the admitting room and was questioned by a tall black man with a moustache. He siphoned through my wallet looking for my identification and assured me that its contents would be safe with him. Then, I was told to wait in the lobby. Sports highlights were on television. I remember seeing a women's professional golf recap. The next thing I knew I was spinning around in a circle. The hospital staff saw this as odd behavior, and they rushed me into a vacant room. They forced me onto a mattress and stuck syringes of Ativan and Haldol into my bloodstream via my hamstrings. I was out for good.

Of all of my hospitalizations this 2001 visit to County was the least memorable in my mind. I remember two black staff members that I thought looked like pro players from the Dallas Cowboys. There was a patient who looked like the actor Randy Quaid. He and I used to exchange candy, a common practice then and into the future. Fun-sized Snickers were his top choice while I liked Dots.

There was also a neighboring patient competing with me for this fine, well-dressed female patient. Her dad was a fire chief, and my uncle was a New York firefighter. We had something to talk about there, but she showed little interest. One day for recreation we were invited down to the hospital's bowling alley. Our staff leader did not bowl. I bowled a 137 good for best out of all of the patients- not bad for someone that had not bowled in ten years.

Social workers, in a program called Sail, made an agreement with my parents that upon release I would not be allowed to live at home. For two weeks I lived at the Milwaukee County Respite House on South 68th Street. This happened to fall during the time of the September 11th airplanes crashing into the World Trade Center. I shared the home with a few roommates- some had been crack co-caine addicts now in recovery stages. One night they were bragging about it including our staff member. I thought to myself: where the hell am I? Then after two weeks the County budged. They said that it was okay for me to live at home with my parents as long as I was actively looking for an apartment.

I finally found an apartment in October. It was on Albion Street near Brady. Unfortunately, it was a studio apartment. My rent was $360 per month. Remember how Dr. Kay Jamison said that a severe manic episode is often followed by severe depression. Well, my resi-dence on Albion marked one of my most depressed times in life. I lived right on the bus line with a stop on the nearby corner, so I had to listen to the roar of the green machine's engine and brakes while trying to sleep. Also, the heat was not regulated efficiently. The ra-diator would emit its last warm steam around midnight, and then I would wake up cold in the morning. My refrigerator and freezer were pathetic. I could not even fit a frozen pizza in there. As depressed as I was, I really did not feel like food shopping on a daily basis. I only made contact with three people while staying on Albion. One was the apartment manager. Another was a bipolar high school friend that I played soccer with back in middle school, but he moved out when

I moved in. The third was a young lady in the hallway. She had been doing laundry and walked by my door showing a beautiful array of bras and panties. Luckily, I got out of my lease on Albion because somebody was looking for an apartment and he happened to be the manager's friend.

Columbia Hospital
Summer 2002

THE CIRCUMSTANCES OF my arrival, though police-related, were far different and comforting than in 2001 at County. A local police chief served as my chauffer to Columbia Hospital. We would cross paths again during a later hospital visit, and my opinion of him would change. I had not been there long before I was directed to my bedroom. There was an array of magazines on the night table alongside my bed ranging from "Time." "Sports Illustrated" to "National Geographic" among others. I was manic, so reading concentration would be a problem. Nevertheless, good stories existed in these magazines including an excellent one about Lewis and Clark. Did you know that Clark suffered from depression?

Columbia's staff was second to none. I was treated like a king during my hospital stay. Also, I found a new psychiatrist who visited me there. I remember mooning him there when I was unhappy. Anyway, he has a husband and wife practice not too far from the Downer Movie Theater on Milwaukee's East Side. I had a male Latino nurse during the beginning of my stay at Columbia. I had barely been there an hour before I was playing him at ping pong. I am not too shabby at the game and used to have delusional thoughts that I was Forrest Gump. In addition, this particular nurse fixed me up with cranberry juice mixed with Sierra Mist- refreshing for the Milwaukee summer heat.

One of Milwaukee's best surgeons happens to be a close family friend. He used to visit me in the hospital because his patients are at Columbia, and he just so happens to be a very compassionate person. During my stay I had waning maria, and my creative thinking led to an artistic nature. I produced numerous pictures having a common theme. Over the years, especially after having worked at Lincoln, I developed an appreciation for the US Military. At that time, I used to think that I knew Morse Code. My doctor friend had been a medical officer in the Navy, so he particularly enjoyed my drawings of Navy submarines. I remember trying to design a state-of-the-art underwater weapon for our military. Earlier that summer I bought the military branch flags except for the Coast Guard. I decorated my workout area in the basement from left to right: Army, Navy, Air Force and Marines. Back in the summer of 1998 I tried getting into the military except for the Air Force at a time when I was training for and running marathons three consecutive years. I was in the best physical shape of my life. The Marines wanted me, but my mood stabilizer disqualified me.

The close personal care did not stop with my doctor friend and first nurse, for I had another nurse that used to play movies for me. He also would bring me some great chocolate chip cookies. Whenever my parents visited in the evening, this nurse would have a meeting with us to discuss my progress. He boosted my confidence and helped me from falling back into a severe depression. This white nurse also had a memorable look. He had extremely short and curly yellowish-blonde hair looking like that of a black man.

County Hospital Fall 2004

RECOLLECTION OF MY hospital stay at Milwaukee County from mid October to mid November was probably the easiest due to recency. I had been slightly manic for most of the summer because I reduced my Lithium Carbonate from 1200 mg to 900 mg daily. With the summer heat and my activity, the mania built up around Labor Day. Things were going well for me, at least I thought. I had a beautiful Latina girlfriend and had just started a Masters degree studies in urban planning at the local university. In addition, I was working out with weights every other day and running on alternate days. I was becoming a hard body at 205 pounds. I got very serious rushes of energy during workouts. Once I lifted weights for three hours and ten minutes. I had some other comparable workouts. The music of AC/DC, Def Leppard, and Aerosmith inspired me and sent blood rushing to my muscles.

The family support system was not there for me just prior to my relapse on October 12th. My mom was with friends in New York City, and my dad was up at a friend's cottage in Three Lakes, Wisconsin. My dad came home before my breakdown, but I locked him out of the house. He went over to my sister's home in Whitefish Bay and slept there on Monday night. Then he returned the following day and used my sister's key to get into our house. He also took my dog Cooper who I had regrettably forgotten to feed the last day before my mental breakdown.

People did try to warn me of my mania, but I refused to acknowledge their pleas. One of these persons was an extremely influential psychiatrist family friend. He had started up a support group that I regularly attended on Tuesday nights. On a couple of days prior to my breakdown he was trying to convince me that I was manic and that I was going to end up in the hospital if I did nothing about it. I remember not taking him seriously because I was out walking dogs with a neighbor. I did not want to be bothered then because I was out for some peacefulness and solitude.

On Monday night I watched the Green Bay Packers play the Tennessee Titans. It was a hard-fought game with the Titans winning. I was extremely pissed that the Packers had lost. The strange thing about the game was that the Titans were repeatedly tackling the Packers extremely hard on most offensive plays for Green Bay. We had an older RCA television in the basement, so I did not feel too bad about defacing it with the word "Freaks" on the screen due to the Titans' victory. See, I only care about the Packers when it comes to the National Football League. Many Wisconsinites take a similar position as diehard Packer fans.

Little sleep represented that night and previous nights. Sleep and complying with a medication regimen ordered by a doctor are imperative. I had the US Military flags hanging up in order except the Coast Guard. Taped to the Army flag was an 8 by 10 inch picture of former Senator Bob Dole. Likewise, the Navy flag had a picture of Senator John McCain. There were also photos of Colin Powell, Wesley Clark, Wisconsin's Secretary of Administration and the fellow I campaigned for back in 1992, and finally one that President and Laura Bush had sent me. Incidentally, I looked into joining the Navy, Marines, and Coast Guard. The Coast Guard told me that I was ineligible. The Marines told me that I was disqualified due to my illness and my medication regimen. Finally, the Navy never got back to me. It had just been two weeks prior to the date when I withdrew from the Masters of Urban Planning program at the University of Wisconsin-Milwaukee. I wanted to work a job instead of going to college for yet another two years. My Mexican girlfriend inspired me to want to serve as a provider. She lived with her ten-year-old son, and I wanted to be there for them. I had no idea how difficult it would be to land a job. Other doors had been shut! I had tried relentlessly to get a public school teaching job in Wisconsin, and I was denied by most branches of the armed forces.

To complicate matters, I had a major lack of communication with the outside world those last three days before going to County. During my final week I called my firefighter uncle asking him to be on the lookout for public works and teaching jobs in New York. He thought that I just might be over the hump with battles I had been having in my brain. I needed two years of professional experience before the FBI would employ me as an Intelligence Analyst. The thought of working for the FBI was just another aspect of my manic episode. How could they accept an employee with bipolar disorder? I did find out that they might under highly controlled circumstances. I also called my aunt from Long Island, New York. She told me that I was talking about "chickens not hatching" for some reason that I could not understand. I wish she could have given me some stern advice because this was the Saturday before my Tuesday admittance to the hospital.

Either my dad and/or my close psychiatrist friend called the local police Tuesday morning. They came barging into the house with their weapons drawn and told me to lie down on the floor. I still had my hand on the oven handlebar. Inside the oven burning was a printed photo of the Milwaukee Public School principal that had interviewed me as well as a golf club. The police did not like the looks of the club because they could see part of it and saw it as my potential weapon. The cops, four of them, proceeded to shoot me with Taser guns. I could not believe the jolt that I felt. They did not back off. Two cops came up and pepper-sprayed me in the eyes. Finally, the last cop to leave had the audacity to pick me up by the back of the head and slam me into the hardwood floor. This blow severely loosened my right front tooth and broke my nose. Can you imagine the dental work? I received a crown by a nice dentist in one of my support groups. Ten years later the root fractured, and I had a bridge installed by my parent's dentist. The crown was complimentary, but that and the bridge would have been over $6,000. I still feel I was treated with excessive force, but now it is too late to take any legal action. The First Responders arrived, and I remember one gentleman wiping my pepper-sprayed eyes with a damp washcloth.

Next, I was taken to Columbia Hospital by ambulance for face x-rays and an evaluation. The nurses positioned me in an emergency room. My guard was the same local police chief that had driven me to Columbia in 2002. He took the gold chain off of my neck and, after quite some time, got me a cup of ice chips for my eye, nose and mouth. My right eye was already starting to turn purple from the blow I had taken in the kitchen earlier that day. My nose was incredibly sore. My mouth was full of blood. I spit some blood into the ice chips. Immediately my guard took the ice away. We talked about Washington DC and Arlington Cemetery's Tomb of the Unknown Soldier. For a while there, I was thinking that I was the unknown soldier for every battle that I had been through. Before I knew it I was being transferred to County Hospital.

County Hospital is where they take patients without health insurance. A lot of crazy stuff goes on at this hospital as mentioned previously. Some of the hospital personnel were professional. I also had a great roommate. His father used to buy us bottles of Coca-Cola. We would refill them with water and drink the water on the unit. One common reaction to taking psychiatric medications is to drink a lot of liquids. This weakens the effect of the medications. For some strange reason our noses used to get stuffy when we were outside of our room. Probably the germs or lack of cleanliness, but I was no saint myself. Lithium Carbonate has the side effect of excessive thirst and caused dry mouth. I was drinking so much water that I was urinating in bed overnight. Once in the middle of the night after wetting my bed(I pissed all over the floor too)two staff members came in mad and picked up my college sweatshirt and nice pants that got wet. I never saw those clothes ever again.

Twice while at County I was physically assaulted by other patients. First, there was a kid living across the hall from me. He always tried to kiss up to the staff. I made him fully aware that his behavior was annoying. One day, he was hiding behind his door and peeking out every once in a while. Like a dummy or something, I went up to his door. Seconds later he lashed out at me with books slung in a top sheet. The books hit me in the lower jaw but caused no bleeding. The staff made me aware that I could press charges. It was not worth it because this kid was an orphan.

Another time my financial adviser was visiting me. There was this young black woman in a wheelchair. She was a big-time basket case. I was heading into the lounge with my financial adviser, and she jumped out of her wheelchair throwing salt and pepper into my eyes. I could barely see. She really did a number on my right eye. I remember pouring some Gatorade into it.

Three staff members were outwardly helpful. I had a female nurse who did favors for me like get sodas from the kitchen. She and I swapped stories about walking our dogs in Estabrook Park and down at the beach. Then there was a front desk employee that would watch major sporting events with me. He also got me snacks and sodas. Next, there was a visiting nurse from MATC. We shot the breeze about the 1980's and talked about how great the Milwaukee Bucks were under Coach Don Nelson. He also turned me on to a new radio station, 97.3 "The Brew," which plays 1980's hits. In an effort to boost my confidence and outlook for the future, he told me that I still have plenty of time to find a woman and settle down. The month that I was at County was a time of great depression since my Mexican girlfriend never came to visit me. I do not blame her. I scared her off.

The massive number of visitors that I received probably kept my spirits up more than anything. My dog-walking neighbors were one of the first to arrive, and the mother made her delicious, chocolate chip cookies for me. A few friends of my parents' age came to visit also. My best male friend at the time took time out of his day on two or three occasions while I was there. One couple from my childhood neighborhood brought me a plastic jack o' lantern full of tootsie rolls, dots, junior mints, and peanut butter kisses. Poor hygiene often takes place on a mental health unit. Patients go days without showering and shaving. I remember having to ask for a toothbrush. Even with this, all of the candy spelled cavities down the road.

Employment and Volunteering

FROM 1993 THROUGH the summer of 2005 I had worked and volunteered at numerous organizations. In 1993 and 1994 I worked for the local department of public works. From 1995-2001 I worked at golf courses- one year at a country club and six years at a Milwaukee County course both serving on the grounds maintenance crew. From the fall of 2000 to the spring of 2001 I taught at a parochial school called Sacred Heart. Then I turned to the non-profit sector and found a reasonable job with Interfaith Older Adult Programs in January of 2002. Next, I put my best foot forward and sub-taught for three years. I also volunteered at the National Alliance for the Mentally Ill-Greater Milwaukee for over one year early in the 21st Century. Whenever I could not find a job, I made a serious effort despite the depression to make a difference. I volunteered at my church for the winter and spring of 2004. Finally, I was a dairy/frozen food stocker at a grocery store from the fall of 2004 to the spring of 2005.

Working for the local department of public works really opened up my eyes towards policy for this sector of government. After all, roads and sewers etc. are antiquated and must be fixed up at times. I was fortunate enough to work under some of the coolest guys, and there was even a woman that I often chipped wood with in the summer heat. She had the same last name as my favorite professional golfer, and she even tried convincing me that he was her cousin. It took a couple of years for me to find out that she was full of shit. Anyway, we had fun working together. The guys that I worked with in street repair, for the most part, had foul mouths or chewed tobacco. One guy used to sit in the truck and listen to the radio while I worked hard shoveling and smoothing out asphalt for road repair. We used to bug him about his age and nickname. He spent so much time at bars that people called him Barney. He also said he was 36-years-old but said it like "dirty sex." Nevertheless, I have the utmost respect for blue collar America and the backbreaking work required to get jobs done. In addition, my two bosses were cool. They allowed me to take off work some Fridays and Mondays to go fishing in northern Wisconsin and even Minnesota.

Probably my two best friends from the local public works were the mechanics. The Chief Mechanic then was "Mr. Baseball" to me. He and I went to a few games together. He had an orange 1976 Corvette and a Harley. He would later become Chief Mechanic of a nearby fire department. The other mechanic was a friendly guy that gave me advice regarding my outboard motor. He had been a political science major in college and religiously listened to different political commentary on the radio while busy servicing the fleet of trucks, heavy equipment, and police cars. I used to think that most unionized workers were Democrats, but these guys were mostly conservative. They have become more centrist over the years.

Golf course maintenance work is physically demanding and falls into the category of dirty, sweaty work. I got my feet wet at Tripoli Country Club learning how to use different lawn-cutting equipment. I had a great boss at Tripoli who agreed to pay me more since I would be going to college that fall. He really was genuinely interested in what we wanted to do with our lives down the road.

I was assigned a variety of tasks while at Tripoli to break up the monotony. I had three major early morning jobs. I would either cut the tee boxes or greens. I used to rake the sand traps or bunkers(all 90+ of them)with the rake rider. Tidying up by hand was a pain in the ass, but the rake rider did more than 90% of the job and was thrilling. I also had a habit, especially on rainy days with few golfers, of searching for golf balls in the water hazards. One day I found sixty-three of them and these were mostly grade "A" balls. On my last day of work one of my co-workers planted a Titleist Professional ball in a clear creek. When I saw it, I went over to the bank to get closer. That is when Joe sneaked up from behind me and pushed me in. I did not have any change of clothes since I was already wearing rain pants over jeans. That is just one fond memory of working at Tripoli. It truthfully saddened me greatly when my boss was killed a few years later in a highway car crash on Father's Day.

I began working for Milwaukee County in golf course maintenance right after my June 1996 trip to Boston and Cape Cod. I got to see then Boston Red Sox pitcher Roger Clemens pitch a complete game, hit a single, and lead his team to victory. All of this while in the company of my dad, grandpa, and an ex-girlfriend from Ripon College who lived just outside of Boston. Before the game we ate at NoName Restaurant on the docks. I remember sharing a platter of seventy-two mussels with my date and having a bowl of seafood chowder. After the game the four of us went to Durgin Park Restaurant for their famous Indian pudding. After this eventful trip it was time to work under one man and with a racially mixed crew that would change my life forever.

My boss was a six-foot black man with biceps the size of my flexed calf muscles. I grew up a lot between 1996 and 2001. This time period did not make me smarter in terms of my not taking prescribed orders of Lithium Carbonate as referenced to my 2000 and 2001 hospital stays. I did instill in myself a stronger degree of patriotism because he had been through hell as a Marine Corps lance corporal in artillery and ammunition in Vietnam. He ran a tight ship, and you got canned if you were not on board. His reputation for firing employees was notorious. He was not liked by most of his employees- even the regulars that had logged many years of service. We were granted a 9:15 AM break period but sometimes took it early. If he caught us, then he would come into the entranceway of the break room, shuffle his feet, and say, "Dit ain't break time." He never really changed his personality from his military days. I came to the conclusion that much of this fact was probably true for many soldiers and sailors during any battle that the US engaged in over our brief history. The boss and I did not see eye-to-eye that first season in 1996. He would come roaring into the service yard in his yellow truck yelling, "Hey Dow!, How many plugs did you get, huh?" This phrase is used for someone assigned to repairing the greens. Repairing the greens was one of the worst if not the worst job, especially in the summer heat. It was very tedious. Later during my last season of 2001 he would say, "Dow, you are like a surgeon and you are the best at repairing the greens." When I threatened to quit in 1996 due to his "riding my back" so hard he took me aside in his office and told me that I had the potential to be his assistant. It was a constant breaking down of my spirit and building it back up by him and myself. It took a lot of will power to work for this man for six years. He always thought that I wanted to be a teacher, but my 2000 failure had changed that dream. Six seasons of work under this boss for Milwaukee County and I never got promoted to a regular with good benefits. When I asked Johnson if I was up for rehire after six seasons he told me "I did it." Maybe it was like I had passed his test. Today he lives comfortably with two houses. I'll bet the lawns look nice. He had a knack for landscaping.

The crew at Lincoln formed most of the camaraderie in my life during those six years. My 2000 and 2001 hospital stays caused me to lose some of my closest friends. They simply gave up on me. One crew member at Lincoln was pretty heavy, so I jokingly called him Buffy. Still, he was a good co-worker and one of the best on TurfCat mowers used for cutting the rough. We rarely cleaned out the air filter on this type of mower. I remember my boss telling me how to do this. He said, "Hey Dow, you put your finger in there like you would a pussy and go back and forth and up and down." Next, there was a guy some of us called grandpa. He was in his late 40's and still a seasonal maintenance worker. Grandpa and I enjoyed some Milwaukee Brewers baseball games together, but I never got him or anybody from our crew(except one fairly new worker in 1998)out in my fishing boat. We had a microwave in our break room, and grandpa used to fry bologna in it for lunch. I tried his favorite meal one day. It truly was tasty but not much different than a hot dog. The difference between fried bologna and a hot dog was that bologna curls up on the edges and retains the salty juices emitted from the microwave's cooking.

Video Man and Running Back joined our crew later on in my days and nights there. Video Man was studying film in the fall, winter, and spring. On rainy or cold, overcast days he and I played some golf when boss was on vacation. I had played golf in college, and my skills were still honed for the most part. Consequently, Video Man expressed an interest in making a video of me playing golf. It never happened, and Video Man left before the season was over. When I was Nightman he used to swing by after dark, take pretty chicks for golf cart rides, and screw them in the park. Running Back probably had the best sense of humor out of all of them. He and I used to imitate our boss. He was a star high school football player with blazing speed. To this day, I still keep in touch with Running Back and Buffy.

Wacky, Black Panther and GeoMac also had a profound effect on me. Wacky was my assistant boss, so he served as head boss sometimes. I remember when he burned the cd of "Top Gun" for me upon request. Those songs were meaningful to me and fired me up because I wanted to join the Navy in the late 1990's back when I was in peak physical shape. I wanted to become a SEAL. Man was I mixed up. I was studying to become a teacher, my boss did not think that I wanted a career in the park system, and now I wanted in with the armed forces. Stress led to hospitalizations. Wacky used to call my mom to see how I was doing whenever hospitalized and post hospitalization too.

Black Panther always got the best job assignments due to his seniority. I remember how he used to spit out sunflower seeds when cutting the fairways. He also used to repeat words over and over. For example, one time I was changing the cups on the greens and I frustratingly threw the cup cutter towards my motorized cart. It got wedged in between the gas pedal and headed for the Milwaukee River. His response was, "Oh no! The river, the river, the river." He also used to say greens, greens, greens and cups, cups, cups when discussing our daily job assignments. Black Panther lived in a dangerous neighborhood and never seemed to have a rear window to his minivan. Instead, he took heavy duty plastic and used a powerful hairdryer to seal the window area. Only when close up could you tell that it was not glass.

GeoMac was also an assistant boss like Wacky. He praised me more consistently than any other boss. He used to joke with me and say, "Bryan, I got another shitjob for you." He said I was a real good worker and even told me I would make a great regular someday if I wanted it. I often wonder how these guys are doing. I do keep in touch with Wacky every so often.

The lessons learned were abundant while working at Lincoln. I befriended a slew of black golfers and decided that friendship trumped race. This golf course was named after President Lincoln who wrote the Emancipation Proclamation after all. The golf course is located right on the edge of government subsidized housing. The neighborhoods to the West are questionably safe. Two regular golfers became friends with me. One was a city firefighter who used to always encourage me to self-promote myself and look to elevate my status in life. He used to tee off before the starter got there, play nine holes, and then pay for his round and a cup of coffee he enjoyed while smoking a cigarette. He was behind me 100% with my aspirations for the Navy, but he never knew or at least I did not tell him about being bipolar. The other fellow was a black man retired from the AO Smith corporation. He grew up in Georgia and left the farming South for Milwaukee when it was considered one of the nation's manufacturing centers. There was no question he could play. With his unique, off-balance swing he managed to shoot close to even par for nine holes on occasion. I saw him once at the Greater Milwaukee Open and invited him once to spectate at the Western Open just outside of Chicago.

At Lincoln Park Golf Course there was the service yard and the clubhouse where the cooks and starters worked. My boss was married but was fooling around with one of the golf starters. Pretty soon I had her coming on to me. She used to say that she would love to get naked for me and get a hotel room. I preferred not paying for the sex and having it at her place on the West side. She was amazing at deepthroating cock like I had never been a recipient before. We fooled around numerous times. Then she told my boss. I possessed the fact that he was a married man and could use it against him if necessary in the future. This crossing of paths was the only sour note that I left my boss with.

My boss had post-traumatic stress disorder(PTSD)from being shot at and shooting and killing many Vietnamese soldiers. I truly believe that he felt for me having this mental illness which sprouted when I went to DC in 1993 and has never left me since. He also wears two very powerful hearing aids. Once I saw him dip his left pinky finger in battery acid and then into his ear. This goes to show that some soldiers can be part machine if they withstood and survived serious wounds. My boss was not the only man I knew that claimed that he had wires running throughout his body due to battles in Vietnam.

I was employed during the spring, summer, and sometimes fall at Lincoln Golf Course Maintenance Yard from 1996-2001. Working there very early in the morning meshed with my lifestyle because I had been used to rising early to go fishing and play golf. This though was seriously early. My shift was 4 AM until Noon most of the time. I also worked some nights alone. Here I was between the ages of 23 and 28 working early hours and sacrificing a quality social life. I never was much of a drinker but friends would give me a hard time if I did not have a beer in hand. I would rise around 3:30, get ready and leave for work. Three of those six years, 1997-1999, I was adamantly training for the Milwaukee LakeFront Marathon in the fall. For the 1998 race, I started my training in December of 1997 and finished close to qualifying for the Boston Marathon. Sometimes I wonder if rising early and exercising so intensely contributed to my illness getting worse in 2000 and 2001 when I was hospitalized, but I would not exchange those marathon medals for anything. I can tell you one thing. The early morning rise increased my metabolism, and I was able to shed the weight and remain thin until the hospitalization would lead to severe depression. During my running years I could eat three large meals each day or two meals and a bunch of snacks.

I also could treat myself to indulgences like cake, brownies, cookies, and ice cream and not have to worry since I was running close to 50 miles per week.

Teaching at Sacred Heart School in northern Racine marked a time when I finally was hired to teach full-time. I taught 6th, 7th, and 8th grade social studies, literature, health, and religion from October of 2000 to March of 2001. My 7th graders were angels for the most part. The 6th grade boys were rowdy and uncooperative, and most of the 8th graders just did not want to be there. I worked extremely hard to prepare these kids for a quality education. The 6th grade boys used to brag about how they ran the last teacher out. They told me that I was their 3rd teacher of the year, and I only started on October 16th. Something was definitely wrong. The 6th grade boys and 8th grade girls were only interested in forcing me to quit or get fired like the previous two teachers. I remember giving the 6th graders a test on ancient Greece and Rome. They could not even handle it without their notes and/or working in small groups.

Sacred Heart's principal then was a close ally, and he remains as one of my writers for letters of recommendation. He used to tell me that I needed that swagger and not to be afraid to point my index finger at the kids and send them down to his office. Despite my efforts as a new teacher, he told me that I never really got the hang of taking charge. We had an awesome Christmas party for faculty at the Prime Quarter- a place where you get to grill your own steak. My boss gave me a gift consisting of cheese and sausage. He told me how happy he would be when I secured a middle or high school teaching job in the public schools where the salary and benefits were far better than parochial schools.

One of our greatest achievements while at Sacred Heart was 7th grade Colonial Fest. We invited all grades at this K-8 school to come to our room and see displays depicting life in the early American colonies. My students really got to display their creativity. They recreated Jamestown, designed weapons for hunting and defense, displayed beautiful 17th and 18th Century architecture and every student earned an "A." I had them working in small groups. About the only disappointment was that the boys especially destroyed their displays when it was all over. It dawned on me that their younger brothers and sisters could have used them as a guide. Other faculty members told me that it was a "hit" and that I should continue this program in future years.

Like Lincoln, Sacred Heart was demanding for an early riser, and taking medications makes it even more difficult than the average person to get up in the morning. I usually woke up around 5:30 AM to get ready. I would arrive at school shortly after 7 almost fifty minutes before the students. My Indian psychiatrist was prescribing an antidepressant medication called Remeron. This drug caused me to gain weight. It made me hungry, and I ate more than I could handle. One of my 6th grade boys used to jokingly poke me in the belly. Some of these little twerps made fun of me. They had no idea. I went off the Remeron and began exercising at the Wisconsin Athletic Club in downtown Milwaukee on the way home from work.

Some of our actions in 6th grade brought downright pandemonium in the classroom. Two 6th graders loved to eat chalk in front of the class. I did not disallow this because comic relief was needed with this grade. I also used to bring a snack for our 10 AM break. Often I ate clementine oranges. The same two turkeys that ate the chalk also would eat the peel of my oranges. I never did develop that intimidating swagger that the principal had been talking about, but I did give the students a staredown which bothered most of them. In addition, I used to think some of my students were Devil worshippers. When we had group projects in 6th grade, one group full of all troublemakers(a mistake on my part)re-created the "Blair Witch Project." Many of them died in their make-believe final product- a video of them supposedly camping in the woods.

I lost my job at Sacred Heart because of poor judgment. We were coming back from Wednesday morning Mass and one of them kicked me behind the knee in an effort to trip me. I lost my balance and came close to falling. Had I fallen and stayed on the floor, then this kid would have been expelled and I would have retained my job. Instead, I proceeded over to him, picked him up by his shirt collar and told him never to do that again. I informed the principal as to what had occurred after Mass. Evidently, the boy's parents came in the next day to talk to the principal. He took a lot of heat and succumbed to the pressure. He had to let me go. Fortunately for the student, I had just signed off for him to get a free pass to nearby Six Flags Great America based on his reading quantity. I bet he never did that much reading.

In the spring of 2001 I worked for the Wauwatosa School District as a substitute at-risk educator. My supervisor was very friendly and had a great deal of patience. My responsibility involved monitoring two young men who had gotten in trouble at their respective schools. One stole more than $10,000 worth of computer equipment. He was easy to manage because he followed through on his schoolwork and met deadlines to finish off the year. The other guy had threatened to kill three of his classmates and required much more effort and skill on my part. He was mad at the world and very rebellious. Still, he managed to complete more than ¾ of his assigned work. The district liked me so much, thanks to my supervisor, that they extended an interview for a high school job. I was very sharp at this interview. My answers to questions would naturally segway into their next question. They hired the other candidate because he had the alternative education license which I did not possess. I spent a month in the hospital that summer and did some sub teaching in the fall.

From January of 2002 until mid July of that same year I worked for Interfaith Older Adult Programs as an Activities Assistant at Wilson Park Senior Center. There was also a female Activities Assistant. We never saw eye-to-eye, and thank God our responsibilities rarely overlapped. Her main responsibility included designing the calendar for senior center activities. She was better with the computer and knew how to format the calendar unlike me. My job duties consisted of making flyers for virtually all of the programs, teaching indoor and outdoor golf classes, stocking up the soda machine, working with guest speakers, serving as liaison to the computer instructor, counting money from the kitchen every day and recording it, and mingling amongst the seniors making sure they had everything they needed.

The computer instructor was close to my age and very pretty. I will refer to her as the "Cinnamon Girl." I could tell that she was just as horny as I was for a few reasons. First, she had two kids but had never been married. Here is the kicker. She and I were in an office alone that was normally used by the absent volunteer coordinator. She was getting close to me, so I told her that her black and red shirt was beautiful. Her response was that she wore the shirt often enough, but then she told me that she had matching panties and a bra. I desperately wanted to get it on right then and there. At the very least I could have asked the "Cinnamon Girl" on a date. I did have the green light. Since she had two kids I knew that her pussy would be nice and loose and probably shaven(Hey, this is the 21st Century!). All of this came to my mind in hindsight and not quick enough. I am sure that I could have been the recipient of some juicy cocksucking, and I'll bet she was a pro-again, possibly the thought process going through my bipolar mind. Later that summer I fell ill, and my mental state must have scared her. Years later she unfairly had some influence in kicking me off the volunteer team at her organization.

My health was a factor for some of the time at the senior center. There were days that I felt so depressed that I had to just lie down in the computer lab before anyone arrived. I also started an addiction to soda. In our machine we did not even sell the cans of Sunkist lemonade and orange, so they just remained in the machine. Soon I was drinking them and must have finished off a case in one week. Some of the active, elderly women used to make sandwiches and sell various food items in the center's kitchen. Most items were complimentary for me and, if not, I stole some. I was the only guy working there besides one of the maintenance workers. I would have to say that my health was questionable in the early winter, improved in spring, and deteriorated in early summer when I really got the "hots" for the "Cinnamon Girl." I remember inviting her and her two kids up to my lake cottage for the 4th of July. She said that it was short notice and probably not a good idea to have her baby girl around water. The following week at work she brought me some fresh baked snickerdoodle cookies from the kitchen. She asked me if I was feeling all right. That same day I was sent to go to the grocery store to pick up vanilla ice cream and 2-liters of root beer for root beer floats for the following day. I remember being afraid to drive to the store, so I walked over there and returned with my arms full of groceries. My boss kept asking me that afternoon if I was okay. She sent me home with a piece of apple pie for myself and another for my dad. I would never return to Wilson Park Senior Center as a full-time employee. In the future I would teach golf classes there in the summer part-time.

Three years of my life were devoted to part-time substitute teaching. I filled in for regular teachers at the following districts: Whitefish Bay, Shorewood, and Fox Point-Bayside. I absolutely hated getting phone calls at 5 AM to sub that same day, but I did catch a break with Hawthorne High School.

I had been doing a great job at one of the middle schools and Hawthorne High School. A vacancy occurred for the "building sub" position at the high school. I got it. This meant that now I would arrive at the high school thirty minutes before the students and automatically have a sub position for the day. Some days were busier than others, and I may have found myself filling in for two or three teachers. The job went well until one afternoon when I subbed for a French teacher.

There were two girls flirting with me especially after the lesson plans had been followed and only took half of the hour. I told the class to just sit quietly and stay busy. The two flirting girls asked me if I like being with two girls at a time. I sunk from my professional status and asked the girls if they meant ménage a trois. Obviously, this was the wrong thing to do. The girls hounded me and made me feel uncomfortable. I thought about sticking around after school to speak with the regular French teacher or even telling one of the assistant principals. I did nothing positive. Instead, I stooped down to the girls' level and played their game. One of the girls liked to pull on my gold neck chain. I told her to stop, but she still felt it on later occasions.

When I had lunch duty in the cafeteria I used to "shoot the breeze" with a few guys who knew the two girls. I ended up getting in trouble with the administration and lost my job. I reported to the local police station the next day, and the officer was fair and kind. He said that this should be a lesson to me and did not press any charges. Losing my job hurt emotionally and financially. I was earning $100/day at the end of my assignment at Hawthorne High School.

Finding and securing a paying job can be rather difficult for people with a mental illness. This has been the case for me, so I have volunteered much in my spare time. I volunteered with the National Alliance for the Mentally Ill or NAMI doing things like office work: running errands with the administrators, answering phones, putting address labels on mail, and breaking down boxes for the dumpster outside. One time I completed a lengthy spreadsheet assignment worthy of a paid employee. The volunteers and paid staff were so nice at NAMI that they made me feel worthy. There were always good snacks and drinks for the volunteers. During my two years there I developed a good relationship with the director and social worker. We kept in touch until administration changed a couple of years later. They are thrilled that I'm writing this book. I respected them because they do such meaningful work promoting better lives for people with mental illness, their families, and other loved ones.

I also volunteered at the United Methodist Church of Whitefish Bay working in their office. There I catalogued books, straightened up the sanctuary, wrapped toys for children, sealed envelopes, used the paper cutter, and made photocopies. Everyone working and volunteering there was so sweet. They sent me a birthday card with all of their signatures, and they verbally told me how much they enjoyed me working with them.

Faith-Based Community Support Groups

PROBABLY MORE THAN anything besides my grim determination, faith-based support groups allowed me to cope with my mental illness. For the most part, I belonged to two of them. One was at a Holy Family Catholic Church while the other was at the local United Methodist Church. Both are located in Whitefish Bay. Both groups allowed me to grow spiritually in the company of others. I am far more spiritual five to ten years later, no doubt, because of these groups.

Holy Family Parish support group has been meaningful to me, but we only held meetings no more than twice per month. Everyone was much older except one man who was two years younger. Our group, "Faith in Recovery," was led by a man who took four years to become a deacon. He was a remarkable guy who genuinely cared about each and everyone one of us in the group. He visited me twice while I was in the hospital, and one time he brought a bunch of Panera pastries. I shared them with friendly and eager patients.

The group's founder was a seventy-year-old psychiatrist who was groundbreaking in his belief that there was such a high demand and need for faith-based support groups throughout the Milwaukee area. Other churches have followed his lead, so there has been some recognizable growth. In addition, he has been like a third grandfather to me; maybe more a godfather. He treated me to dinner about once per month and still does when I am in Milwaukee. We enjoyed different ethnic restaurants like Tres Hermanos, Peking Palace, Hop Sheng, Thainamite, and EE-SANE Thai. Before he moved into this elaborate retirement facility, he used to invite me to swim in his backyard pool. Once, when he was on a short vacation, I looked after his dog and cat and spent a few nights there. Our relationship has been very strong since the turn of the 21st Century.

There was also a dentist at Holy Family. He was a very generous man because he put a crown where the police officer back in 2004 had slammed my face into the hardwood floor. This did not come easy, for he did about five temporary crowns before the timing was right to use the porcelain one. He also had assistants clean my teeth and drill and fill a few cavities. My only charge was the crown at a reduced price. All in all, $3,400 worth of work was done with me only paying $275.

Another gentleman a bit older than my father has become a close family friend. His daughter, very close in age to myself, also has bipolar disorder. He and my parents always have swapped ideas as to how to live with their mentally-challenged children. He is somewhat of a father figure. We have probably gone fishing together more than a dozen times. I am now jealous of him living right near Lake Michigan and fishing northern Wisconsin while I live in a desert. We keep in touch two or three times per month. As with most of my Wisconsin friends of all ages, I usually reach out and make the calls but they usually are happy to hear from me. The older friends and I have a core group(55-85-year-old mostly male)that returns calls more promptly than the younger ones.

The United Methodist support group met every Wednesday. It was started by a woman with bipolar disorder that knew the founder of "Faith in Recovery" at Holy Family Parish. We named our ministry "Courage with Christ." My favorite time of the year to attend these meetings took place between Labor Day and early spring when there was a bountiful dinner in fellowship hall for only $5. We were blessed to have such a creative gourmet cook at UMC-Whitefish Bay. There were good socializing times also. The group started out consisting of mostly middle to upper aged individuals, roughly forty to seventy, but fizzled fairly quickly to just 3-9 people. The last two years of the ministry it was just my folks and a successful actuary with bipolar disorder that has kept in touch with me on a 3-4x/month basis whether by phone or email. He has been a spiritual mentor as well as a sounding board for Wisconsin sports and recipes in cooking. When the group first started there were far more participants admitting to have a mental illness than at "Faith in Recovery." There were two teachers both having anxiety that joined us for maybe the first year on and off. One stayed on longer. The Spanish teacher was genuinely interested in me and my hopeful progressions. It excited her greatly when she heard that I was embarking on the endeavor of writing this book. Another group member did not last long due to her health. She developed lung cancer having never smoked in her lifetime. It spread to her bones. I felt for her schizophrenic son, and we got together a couple of times for dinner and just talked. In both of my support groups, the participants were far more religious than me. Both groups allowed me to grow spiritually. They ended with either the Lord's Prayer or the Serenity Prayer. I do not feel the greatest about "forgiving our trespassers" because I believe that the dean of American University and the Milwaukee Public Schools principal went well beyond their authority using their positions of power. My current pastors have told me that I must forgive. In time I will.

My Love Life 1993-2004

I WAS DIAGNOSED with bipolar disorder in 1994, and I dated a girl from rural Wisconsin during the summers of 1993 and 1994. Why do I refer to her as Country Girl? She lived on Log Cabin Road in Fond Du Lac County's Kettle Moraine. The land around where she lived was formed when, about 10,000 years ago, glaciers melted forming a bunch of lakes and rivers. Country Girl was absolutely beautiful and very athletic. Could I turn the clock back to the summers of 1993 and 1994 I would say to her, "Your breasts are like gazelles, twin deer feeding among lilies(Song of Songs 4:5). She had brownish-blonde hair and stood 5'8" blessed with a zest for the outdoors. Horseback riding was one of her favorite hobbies. She was waiting tables at Silver Springs Inn when I met her. It will never slip my mind what we had for dinner. I had one of my favorites: barbecued pork baby back ribs. My parents both had their trout specialty. I waited after dinner to get her name, some info, and her phone number.

The summer of 1993 was fun, and I felt lucky to be hanging out with Country Girl. We went hiking numerous times on the Parnell Tower Trail in the Kettle Moraine State Forest. I took her fishing in our red canoe. She caught a big crappie and took it off the hook all by herself- my kind of woman! We also used to go out on dinner dates to places like Chissy's Pub and Grill. I liked her mom and step-dad. Her mom made the best lemonade. When the summer was coming to a close we promised to write. The last night we were together I held her in my arms on the front lawn at my parents' seasonal lake home. I swear I saw a shooting star. She was in my thoughts the few nights before my breakdown in DC. Before heading to DC I had been staying at my grandma's house on Long Island, New York. There I wrote and then mailed a three-page letter to my summer sweetheart Country Girl. After returning home she told me that she got the letter and that she wrote back to my American University mailing address. Her letter was never forwarded to me, and that pisses me off to this day! I wonder what she had said in her letter- her thoughts, feelings, and emotions.

Despite my 1993 breakdown, Country Girl gave me another chance during the spring and summer of 1994. I remember telling her in the spring that my mom had extra tickets to August's Billy Joel/ Elton John Concert at Milwaukee County Stadium. She wanted to buy one for her mom after I had invited her to go with me. That summer we also hiked and went out for dinner. One July night she and her brother and I went to go see "Forrest Gump" at the Kohler Memorial Drive Theater. That was probably my favorite movie and Gump kind of reminded me of myself. When we got back to the lake cottage I asked her brother to give Country Girl and I some time alone. It was then that I presented her with sterling silver earrings that had her birthstone in them. She wore them to the concert later that summer in August and looked magnificent. The concert was awesome, but we were not that affectionate except when Billy Joel played "Piano Man" we had our arms around one another. Like 1993 the summer had to come to a close. Again, I held her in my arms on the front lawn and told her that I did not want to lose her by going back to Wooster. Had I transferred to Ripon then, I would have been a half hour's drive from where she was going to college. In hindsight, I was a fool because I did end up eventually transferring to Ripon one year later but would have another breakdown before then.

Just as a point of interest and a final note on this relationship, Country Girl from my life story currently lives in a suburb of Dallas called Flower Mound. She is married and has one son and is very successful professionally having written books and been a motivational speaker. She visits family in Wisconsin each year for Father's Day. I am sure she does not forget where she came from, but she is most likely happy to also consider herself a Texan. Way to go Samantha Summer! I will never forget where I came from as I relax here in my study and ponder our flags and my picture standing next to a statue of the young Abraham Lincoln on the campus of Ripon College.

While at Ripon College I briefly dated a woman that had the nickname "Tank." She was as tall as me and athletic. She had the reputation of having beaten up some of the football players. Tank was from the Boston area and wanted to become a veterinarian. She was really gentle with me unlike the football player. We used to snuggle in her dorm room listening to Elton John's "Tiny Dancer." My parents had come up for Parents Weekend, and they brought my dog Jonesy. She had a soft cast on one leg because she had strained some ligaments removing rocks from the lake at their seasonal home. Tank was super excited to see my dog, so she was a little rough with her. Eventually, Tank told me that it was not going to work out between us. The most fun we had together took place more than a year later in late June when, while visiting Boston and Cape Cod, my grandpa, dad, Tank, and I went out for fresh seafood and sat in the second row at a Boston Red Sox game.

Tank was not my only girlfriend while at Ripon. I briefly dated a redhead nicknamed carrot-top by some of the fraternity jerks. She was a sweetheart and worked as a residential assistant. We used to cuddle and watch movies at her place. One of my hall mates had told me that he thought she was cute but had bad breath- maybe even chronic like halitosis. I took notice of it, and our relationship faded over time. She really was a sweetheart though and from the East Coast like Tank.

From the summer of 1996 until the summer of 1999 I only had mistresses. They worked at Lincoln where I was employed, but they were in the clubhouse. I worked in the service yard, but these women provided services in their own way. One in particular used to get me soda for free and bring me good food. Not before long, I was going to her efficiency apartment and we were engaging in sexual relations. We would set up the date on the phone. By the time I arrived she would pop in a XXX movie and we would basically copy what was done in the movie. She gave awesome blowjobs. Often times, I would cum in her mouth. She would just go to the bathroom, spit it out, and come back for round two. One time she climbed on top of me and just would not get off. She was determined to fuck me silly. I remember one of our last times, she let me screw her doggie-style. I remember feeling like a porn star pumping away as the two of us moaned. This was about as hardcore as it could get. In retrospect, I think my bipolar pattern of sexual promiscuity was shining during these years.

During the spring and summer of 1999 and 2000, I taught group golf lessons at Doyne, Dineen, and Noyes County parks. I started dating one of my students whom I will call the Experimenter. She was a middle school biology teacher and had all kinds of different rodent animals in her basement. The Experimenter had a best woman friend in the golf class who was married and had three kids. I followed their softball team that summer and gave them moral support. She was never going anywhere as a golfer. She lacked the patience and gave up too easily like many other novices. Our nightlife together was very interesting. I ended up carrying her drunken body twice that summer out to my car. She just did not seem to know when to quit and would drink herself into oblivion. I thought that I was supposed to be the one with the mood disorder. I could have violated her in multiple ways after driving her drunken ass home from the bars, but instead I got her bed ready, tucked her in, and left for home once she was sound asleep. I moved on but did stop by to visit when I was teaching at-risk kids for the Wauwatosa School District. She lived close by.

I had another fling while working at the Wilson Park Senior Center. She was a maintenance worker, so she was very tough and handy. I am going to call her Catwoman because she had nine cats living at home. She bred them and showed them at large state and private competitions. Unfortunately, her house smelled like cats. Whenever I slept over I used to wake up nauseous from the smell of all of the litter boxes. The highlight of our relationship took place one winter evening when she and I and two buddies went to a Milwaukee Admirals hockey game. We had passes for a pre-game supper with Admirals personnel, but the climax of the night took place at half-time. Catwoman and I went down the corridors of the Bradley Center until we finally arrived at the Zamboni Machine. She got to ride the Zamboni back and forth with its driver and clean the ice. Besides the cats, the only reason I broke up with Catwoman was to pursue the Cinnamon Girl.

In 2004 during the summer and early fall I dated the second woman that I wanted to spend the rest of my life with. She was a lovely Latina woman who was born roughly two hours south of Mexico City. The reason I had my eyes set on her was because she had been my server for about eight years at Tres Hermanos Restaurant on Lincoln Avenue. She worked very hard there as well as at a plastics corporation during the third shift. Miss Latina had a great body with pretty, narrow dark eyes and was a natural at customer service. At thirty-three years of age, she had an eighteen-year-old daughter in Arizona and lived with her ten-year-old son. She had never married, so I took an open-minded view on our relationship. She wanted to make a baby with me. Her hopes were to have a small wedding with family. She and her son came over for dinner and they came up to my parents' seasonal lake home. She always would hug and kiss my parents upon leaving. When we went hiking in the woods, she got bit on the ass by a mosquito. She let me scratch it, and oh what an ass it was! She had her doubts about me because she did not think that I could be seriously interested in a woman like herself who was going to be a grandmother at thirty-three. That did not matter. I wanted to be with her, but we broke up abruptly when I had the altercation with the local police and ended up in the hospital. Miss Latina was one in a million to me. She looked like the woman in The Tubes music video "She's a beauty, one in a million girls one in a million girls."

I wanted to be there for her because she took on much in life-raising a son, paying three car payments, and renting a duplex house all represented major responsibilities. I gave her son the coolest black remote control Corvette as a gift. He said thank you but still seemed to like his hand-held video game system more. On Miss Latina's birthday, September 5th, we went to Fiesta Garibaldi Restaurant by the Brewers' baseball stadium. She ordered me three margaritas, but they were so weak compared to Tres Hermanos that I probably could have driven home one-handed. After dinner we went to a nearby park and she proceeded to tell me that her last boyfriend had been a state trooper who committed suicide with a gun right in front of her. It was not before long that I became increasingly manic. I had reduced my Lithium Carbonate from 1200 mg to 900 mg, and I was exercising vigorously. I was cross-training with weights one day and running the next while starting a graduate school program. When I ended up in the hospital, it was just a matter of time before she would no longer be with me. It still hurts. I do not blame her and have moved on. She already had the added pressure of her mom and older sister taking medications for depression. She told me this on her birthday. It would have been the perfect time for me to open up to her and share some of my health history. I was afraid that I would lose her if I told her about any of my personal health. Instead, I lost her anyway. I did not take our break-up well, blamed myself, and then reverted to depression. This kind of reminds me of Bon Jovi's "You give love a bad name," "Shot to the heart and you're to blame. You give love a bad name."

Maybe I should have sought out relationship counseling at this time. Instead, I relied on close friends to help me sort out my messed-up life. By 2005 I was ready again for a relationship like Country Girl or Miss Latina. I still frequented Tres Hermanos where Miss Latina was a server and tended bar. Except for one time when she told me that she wished the best for my family and I, she treated me like a stranger in the crowd.

In May of 2005 I met a woman on MySpace from El Paso, Texas that would later become my wife. She had been in the Navy for ten years and was currently a special education teacher. That summer in July she inspired me to start writing this book. I wrote more than half of the memoir that July. Sure, I missed out on many great summer activities, but it allowed me to get my issues off of my chest and cope with them even better.

Family Life

FAMILY COMES FIRST period! I learned this the hard way because I was not fully aware of how much my parents especially were sacrificing for me. My dad had to leave work on numerous occasions to check on my health and attend doctor appointments. My mom chauffeured me around to my medical appointments. She could not hold a job at times because taking care of me came first. Most of these times were post hospital stays when I was weakest and lacked energy. In the early stages of my mental illness my mom had to bring my medications along with a cup of water to my bedside. Otherwise, the psychiatrists feared the risk of me being non-compliant. When I was a patient at Georgetown, I was in a strange place in a fairly unfamiliar city. Honestly, I was scared. My mom made me feel more comfortable by purchasing a Walkman at Georgetown so that I could listen to good music like Eric Clapton. My dad chaperoned other patients and I on walks around the exterior of the hospital. I do not like to dwell on family life mainly because it has been so painful and enduring for them.

Once while in Boca Grande, Florida I blacked out and fell on a fishing pier. My mom immediately got on the phone with my first psychiatrist at Milwaukee Psychiatric Hospital. He had been inundating me with sedating drugs. While at every single hospital my parents were there for me. They would visit at least three times per week. Still, my dad and I had never been the same since 1993. He wanted me to be more than a teacher. Then he wanted me to be a teacher followed by a teaching assistant. From 2002 until the present he has just wanted me to get a job. Nobody, except myself and maybe my wife that sees me on a daily basis, can begin to understand the interference going on in my brain. Nevertheless, my folks have always been there for me when I have been financially up against the wall. From 1994 to 2012 I could have been living off of Social Security Disability

Insurance(SSDI)due to my disabling disorder, but I chose at least to try and work. I have lost a handful of jobs due to my condition. Therefore, I choose now to write and be my own boss. I have been on SSDI since December of 2012 and can contribute to monthly bills and necessities to some degree, but I spend more every month than I receive in my government check. If I did not have my wife, then I would be living on government subsidized housing, buying food from food banks, and be receiving food stamps. My wife is a Godsend!

My older sister has been greatly impacted by my illness. Currently raising teenagers, my sister and brother-in-law have shielded their children away from me. It is as if I am not even an uncle. I guess that when I verbally fight with family like in resulting 2004 and 2009 hospitalizations this negatively affects and hurts various family members. Since I have been trained to be an educator I am naturally inclined to want to know how my niece and nephew are doing in both academics and athletics. They are both "A" students as well as excellent soccer players. They play year-round in WI. However, I receive most of the details from my parents because my sister's shielding has basically terminated our relationship. Politics has also gotten in the way. My Wisconsin family is far more liberal than I am. They get their daily news from MSNBC while I get mine from FOXBN or the Fox Business Network. Neither of us watch a lot of TV though but probably more than we did 10-20 years ago reason being: my folks are both retired although my dad does some contract work and I have a fair amount of idle time as I take breaks from my writing. On a final note, my folks spend all major holidays with my sister and her family. I know this occurs since she only lives five minutes from them and that they are grandparents. It would be nice for them to visit us once on Christmas or Easter. They have already been to El Paso for Thanksgiving but never on the actual day. I guess I should not complain. My WI family has potential for more improved relations, especially since my mother is currently fighting a battle with cancer. I definitely did not want relations to improve due to an illness, but the fact is they will improve steadily. On another note, my parents and I have communicated via telephone almost every day. My mother is the more social type while my father is usually quiet and serious.

My current friends ranging from 40-85 years old have visited me in the hospital over the years. While therapeutic, it only would increase my desire to get released from those institutions. Various friends would visit and reminisce and bring cookies, Gatorade, other drinks, candy, fishing magazines, and other sports magazines. I appreciated the reading material, but all of the medications made it very difficult to concentrate. I would find myself viewing the pictures and that's about it.

One friend in particular has displayed sincere loyalty towards me. I could always count on Jim to visit three or four times, only on weekends due to his work schedule, during my various hospital stays. He would visit me in the unit strutting his stuff showing off his University of Michigan sweatshirt- the undergraduate school he attended. Jim has been such a loyal friend finding some time for me when he currently has three kids ranging from nine to fourteen. One time I somewhat crossed the line with him and his wife. She was a former Milwaukee Public Schools physical therapist, so my mind told me that she might have been on the side of the principal that had crossed my path during and after my interview. I said some mean things and almost lost a friend. His wife, Annette, has been nothing but gracious to my wife and I. When visiting we get invited to their home for cookouts and other dinners. Once she made the ultimate peach cobbler, and she let me have seconds. Jim is much thinner than me, so drinking soda is okay for him. Still, he always offers me a Coke and I often oblige as a rare and special treat. I keep in touch with Jim, for the most part, on a weekly basis as I do with my other best friend Kurt. I met Kurt in 2006, so he has not been through the thick and thin of my turbulent life like Jim has.

Two relatives, my father's youngest brother and my mother's youngest sister, have been there for me for advice and a lending ear. This is especially true from May of 2017(the month of their birthdays) until the present day. They both live in NY, but my unlimited long distance phone service allows us to communicate. They always return my calls as we do a good job of keeping in touch. My uncle and I talk two to three times per week mostly about family, especially my ninety-two-year-old grandfather. He supports me in my writing while we discuss modern political issues. My aunt and I talk to one another two to three times per month, however, each call lasts over an hour. Both my aunt and uncle are very supportive in regards to all of the crap that I have been through in the past twenty-five years. My uncle did not find a steady career until his early thirties. He is a firefighter. My aunt took care of her mother like a nurse would for the last ten years of her life. She tends to this massive and blessed garden during three seasons each year and has found her niche. Both have been loyal to their parents and helpful over the years, and they have worked hard to find their calling. I guess the best way to describe them is a two-way street of moral support.

Pets in my Life

TWO FOUR-LEGGED FUR ball friends, Jones and Cooper, have played a critical role in my healing and feeling better in difficult times. Jones was our family dog from 1987 to 1999. She was a black and white English Springer Spaniel. Even though she was a family dog, she would usually follow me around seeking some adventure. My mom handled her health maintenance and usually fed her. Sometimes with other family members, friends, and sometimes alone, I would take Jones hiking on the great trails of the Kettle Moraine North where Country Girl and I hiked during the summers of 1993 and 1994. My mom took a wonderful picture from behind Jones and I while walking the Parnell Tower Trail. I have a picture frame holding three different pictures in stages, and it still rests on my bedroom wall in Wisconsin.

Jones, like most spaniels, loved to be around lakes. I used to take her fishing in the canoe and rowboat. Usually the boats would have some water in the bottom where she would fall asleep and snore after a tough day of swimming. She always expected us to view her as the Queen. She would burrow underneath the covers of family members' beds to stay warm during the winter. My next-door neighbor was in high school when I was in 8th grade. He used to yell to Jones from the end of the block while walking home from school. She would get all excited. Jones was also a fantastic swimmer. She would dive underwater at our lake cottage and remove rocks and freshwater clams. My mom used the bigger rocks for a border in her garden because Jones facilitated this by carrying the rocks up to the top of the bluff. There is no doubt that Jones lifted my depression in '93 and '94. I would not have severe depression again until 2000, and Jones had already gone to doggie heaven because cancer cut her life short.

I remember her last days so well. I had initially discovered a "ball" of fur underneath her chin and close to her chest. My mom and I took her to the veterinarian to have her checked out. The first examination was positive, but then the head vet examined Jones. He said she had cancer. It would only be a matter of time before she would pass on. We had to get her a special type of food that looked like corned beef hash. During her last few days she had a lot of mucous in her eyes. Somebody told us that this was a sign she was crying. My parents and I knew it was time to take her to the hospital when she refused to eat her favorite silver dollar pancakes. We took her in her bed to have her put to sleep. Only I stayed in the room for the euthanasia with the vet. He told me in detail about the lethal injection and was pretty convincing that this was for the best. When the vet inserted the poison into her forearm she let out a big moan and moved her head from one end of the bed to the other. Her heart that had been so full of energy and love stopped beating.

My family was without a dog for nine months. In November of 1999 I took it upon myself to drive northwest of Plymouth and buy another black and white springer. The little guy cost me $200. Females were $300, so I chose the cheaper male. He had a pink spot on the inside of his nose that made it look like a booger. I named him Cooper after three Coopers: the writer James Fenimore Cooper, the actor Gary Cooper, and the Milwaukee Brewers' first baseman from the 1980's Cecil Cooper. This dog follows me everywhere I go. He rested in a chair in the study while I typed my memoir in 2005. Since it was July, he was probably dreaming about going to the beach or the cottage. Cooper also removes rocks from lakes for a hobby. He loves chasing minnows. Once a crayfish attached to his snout pinching him. I have no regrets about buying Cooper, but I have put him through quite a lot with my 2000, 2001, 2002 and 2004 hospitalizations. He acted very excited when I would return from the hospital having no clue what hell I had been through. Once I took Cooper to Lincoln Golf Course Service Yard to meet my boss and co-workers. When Cooper met my Marine Corps boss in his office he immediately lay down on his belly I think as a sign of respect. My boss liked him.

Chronic depression results in much sleeping due to a lack of energy. When I was in the recovery stage after hospital stays Cooper was right alongside of me every fragile step of the way. He did not beg for walks and seeking adventure. He just made the most of them because they were less frequent. My mom would also take Cooper on adventures when I did not feel up to it. Cooper lived 15 ½ years. For the last 3 years of his life I was living in Texas. He hardly recognized me when I would visit in June and July each summer. He was also euthanized because his rear legs' arthritis had gotten so bad and he was losing capability of bodily functions. I loved the guy like he was my son, but I think he was more like a brother that I never had.

Politics in my Life

MY LOVE FOR politics began when I read Hedrick Smith's "The Power Game" which talked about the ins and outs of what occurs in Washington DC. I read this book my senior year in high school for a very demanding government teacher. Then, I decided to major in political science at the College of Wooster. I worked on various political campaigns from local to state assembly to congressional to presidential. This experience gave me a preliminary wealth of knowledge of the process.

In the spring of 1992 my dad ran for the position of village trustee in Shorewood. Our family friends would gather together helping to put up signs and distribute literature. I remember one of my family's best friends lending me a four-wheel drive truck to put up signs in the snow one late March. This type of grassroots campaigning can be the most exciting because there is much uncertainty. 1992 was not the only year. We had to do it again in 1995. Next, my dad was elected village president in 1997. He would serve until 2003.

During the spring and summer of 1992, I volunteered for a young Italian man in his bid for the 5th congressional district seat in Milwaukee and the nearby northern and western suburbs. He had been an academic and athletic standout at Marquette University playing basketball against tough foes like Depaul's Terry Cummings. From Marquette he tried his best to make the New York Knicks squad only to blow his knee out in training camp. Then, he went to Harvard Law School where he would graduate with honors. He landed a job working for Milwaukee's largest law firm Foley and Lardner. My father also worked there from 1971 -2011. The congressional campaign was fun. Mostly fairly young college students and young professionals work hard all day and then get subs or pizza. The candidate and I pounded the pavement in Wauwatosa, Shorewood, and Milwaukee.

This type of work really got my juices flowing. I almost killed the two of us backing out of my driveway. On another day I was in the campaign office on Farwell and North just doing phonebook research, and I overheard our candidate speaking with Ted Kennedy and Dick Gephardt in an effort to raise more money. I could not be there for the primary election since I returned to Wooster. I remember praying that night, but it was not enough. My guy came in 2nd to now Milwaukee's mayor Tom Barrett. My district would now bend even more left for the next eight years and even remain fairly liberal after the election of President George W. Bush. On occasion I kept in touch with my former candidate. I visited him in his office and saw him at some functions. He took a break from private law practice to work as Secretary of Administration under Wisconsin Governor Jim Doyle. He was also busy with family having a wife and four kids.

In 1994 I campaigned for a cool ob/gyn running for state assembly. He had been a graduate of UW-Milwaukee and a real class act as a leader while there. We had to run a very aggressive campaign because expectations were for a dog fight. On a chilly fall day we set out to pound some pavement. The major hotspot was Oakland Avenue near Sendik's grocery store and Walgreens in Shorewood. We positioned ourselves on the west side of the street ready to handout campaign literature to shoppers. The opponent's campaign was on the other side of the street. My candidate decided that he needed a pair of gloves from nearby Harley's men's store, so he left me alone for ten minutes. While he was gone a crazy woman came up to me and wanted to know how my candidate stood on capital punishment. It was not much of an issue unless she meant abortion which I believe should be decided by the courts and not legislators. She made a scene. I could have handled it better myself. The story has a pleasant ending because we won 51% to 49%. He enjoyed several years of successful reelection to the Wisconsin State Assembly.

In the fall of 1996 I lived in Chicago and was studying on an urban studies semester program away from Ripon College. In my spare time I volunteered for the Democratic Party in Lincoln Park. There are very few Republicans living in Chicago downtown area. It's the suburbs and the rural areas in the state that maintain more conservative beliefs. Wow was I ever lucky! I got to have pizza with a bunch of cute women and Mayor Richard Daley's nephew. We did the door-to-door stuff and light office work. There was always a full candy bowl as it was Halloween. One of the highlights took place when President Clinton paid the city a visit. All three candidates that I worked for won their respective races for the US Senate, US House of Representatives, and Illinois State Attorney General. I even served as an election day judge and got paid $105 while meeting some fantastic city workers and senior citizens. The semester went by too fast. I would never wish to live there again.

The 2000 presidential election sparked much interest for my Law and Government students while I fulfilled my student teaching requirement at the high school level. I showed them debates between Al Gore and Bill Bradley, interviews of Senator John McCain, and we did thorough research on the candidates both Democrat and Republican on their respective web sites. My former congressional candidate was supporting Democrat Bill Bradley because he thought Bradley was the most centrist of all the choices. Some might argue that McCain also had centrist stances on the issues even though he ran as a Republican. I read Al Gore's book "Earth in the Balance" and it was well written. I even saw Gore speak at the Pabst Theater in downtown Milwaukee the day after Bill Clinton's mother died. Gore talked at great length about the United Nations. He was so intense or emotional that he scared me. Furthermore, Gore and his wife claimed they cared about people with mental illness. That was only a sound-bite because all Gore cared about was having his influence in the hospital systems of our country like he did from 1993-2000. He did not want to lose that power.

I joined a group of Milwaukee area people in support of Bill Bradley that January. The chief organizers broke us down into fleets that would visit Dubuque and Des Moines, Iowa to lend any and all support in winning the Iowa Caucus. On a frigid, sunny day I drove across Wisconsin crossing the Mississippi River to Dubuque, Iowa. At the campaign office two women were heading the campaign. The most senior leader was unfriendly, demanding, and bossy. She knew nothing about how to treat volunteers, and she had a nasty chain smoking habit. This was nothing like any other campaign that I had volunteered for, but then again this was the big prize- the highest office in the land.

For accommodations I got to stay at this nice family's home. Their son and I had much in common with our golf games. He was playing all around the country on the junior tour or pre-college and succeeding against stiff talent from the South. He was obviously better than me, but we still had good conversations. I woke up in the morning wanting to go for a run. This family lived in a good neighborhood for taking a jog, so I went on an early morning run only to find out that I was locked out of the house. I had to wait until someone came out for the newspaper because I did not want to wake anybody up.

After more phonebook research we were given assignments for our return the following weekend. Those plans faded as I was issued a speeding ticket in Jefferson County. I was depressed, so I returned to Milwaukee and quit working on a campaign in which I had been treated like shit when it came time to work. Bradley's health was a major factor in his loss in Iowa and many other primaries. Deep down I think the media blew it out of proportion because they favored the more liberal Gore. I switched parties and voted for Bush because I thought he and leaders like McCain, a lion in the Senate, were more likely to maintain the US' second to none military power. Also, there were some questionable foreign policy decisions made during Clinton's second term. Colin Powell was at the heart of my backing George W. Bush. When Gore had secured the Democratic nomination, I met with the congressional candidate that I worked for that summer. He tried to convince me that Gore was the most centrist. My experiences working at the golf course made me feel for Powell. My friend said that Powell had been through a lot. I know that

Powell would later on reverse his thinking on some policy matters in favor of Obama, but I believe he stuck to core Republican principles. Even though many claim that Gore was a left-leaning politician like his father, hats off to his research on global climate change- an issue moderate Republicans even often accept.

I hold a dear place in my heart for Colin Powell. He joined the military roughly around the time my Marine Corps golf course boss was drafted or enlisted(I do not even know this today). The former Chairman of the Joint Chiefs of Staff and Secretary of State during 9/11 held an education forum in my home city of El Paso, Texas in July of 2014. It was strange because one of his female staffers called in the spring asking for me when calling to see if I wanted to attend the dinner and event. I had to tell the woman that my wife was a teacher. She said that we were both invited and that it was $50/plate. At this time our phone bill was in my wife's dead grandmother's name and I only had a probationary teaching license and was not working. Only my name, address, and phone number were in the voting re-cords. Why didn't she ask for my wife who had served in the Navy for 10 years and had been a teacher for 6. I declined the invitation saying that our one income and living paycheck-to-paycheck did not allow us entertainment beyond a small group of friends.

I did tell the staffer that Powell should have run for president in the 1990's and that our country would be a lot better off today had he done that. She hammered back that this was an education forum and that it was not about politics. I barked back that education policy ranks right up there in the grand scheme of things. You know connect-ing the dots leaves something for the imagination. In 1993 I failed at interning in DC and experienced the onset of bipolar disorder. From the summer of 1996-2001 I worked under a Marine Corps vet who was disturbed by PTSD. My psychiatrist now believes that I suffer from similar trauma albeit different than from a man that got shot and shot and killed during battle. One year after failing at gradu-ate school I met my future wife online. She served 6 years active, 4 years reserves in the Navy and was stationed at Pearl Harbor for 5 years. We live within shouting distance of the world's largest Army and Marine Corps base in Fort Bliss and kiddy corner to that is Biggs Field Air Force Base.

I ponder the idea as to what I may have experienced going to Powell's education forum. I had already missed him in 1991 for his book signing in Milwaukee. Two strikes on my part. I hope that God willing I will get another opportunity to meet him. Next on my agenda is to get his book and read it.

BOOK TWO

Post 2004 Hospitalization

UPON RETURNING HOME from County Hospital in November of 2004 I had the opportunity to walk my dog every day. I did for a couple of weeks, but then the bad weather hit. We were out there shoveling in early December. Oh! How I hate Wisconsin winters. Once in 1997 I tried landing a good job near Jacksonville, Florida. That might have helped with my winter depression, but I would have also been far from Wisconsin friends and family. Even today 95% of my friends are from Wisconsin.

My support groups kept me going, but I also had a lovely, competent case management worker to help me with structure. She almost always lifted my spirits as she kept tabs on my medications and doctors' appointments. Her schedule was grueling, but I only saw her twice per month. She had Mondays off and worked four ten-hour days. I noticed one day when she leaned over at the kitchen table that she had a large tattoo on her back right above her ass. I thought we would make a great couple. She shared personal information with me like how she had IBS or irritable bowel syndrome. Unfortunately, she lived with her boyfriend.

My psychiatrist and I were bouncing around the idea of adding an anti-depressant to my medication regimen. Studies show that anti-depressants do not help bipolar patients much if any. He always gave suggestions and let me make the final decision. I decided to try Prozac which has the side effect of causing suicidal thoughts. I went to my church volunteer job after my psychiatric appointment one winter day. Then I came home at lunchtime. I had suicidal impulses, and I acted on them. I went to the garage and started my car. Next, I shut the garage door and climbed into my car. I fired up the engine and turned on the vent. I started feeling scared after ten minutes and thought of how much I would miss my dog. It is almost as if Cooper knew what was taking place. He started barking like a madman and I gave up. The carbon monoxide did make me feel dizzy and light-headed though.

My winter days were pathetic for the most part. I turned down the majority of sub teaching opportunities with the Whitefish Bay Schools. I would sleep until lunchtime thereby missing out on the most important meal of the day. I have been told that breakfast is good for metabolism. My mom always wanted me to drink coffee to feel energized, but I do not really like the taste and it makes me feel like I am rotting on the inside. Iced coffee does suit me though. Today I am a moderate coffee drinker. It is difficult for depressed people to find motivation, especially with exercise. Fortunately, I got back on the health kick by running every other day and at least thinking about lifting some weights in the basement. I had a friend that would run with me part-time when his schedule would allow for it. This friend and neighbor has visited me in various hospitals and has been there for me through thick and thin. His mom encouraged me to try to go back to work.

In the spring I developed an interest in working for the US Postal Service. I talked with our veteran mail carrier, and he gave me the run-down. He told me to study for the tests by using the library materials for hopeful postal workers. I obtained two books that contained three of the four types of questions I would see on the civil service exam. On June 3, 2005 I arrived at Serb Hall in the President's Lounge to take the exam. There were so many participants. I ended up sitting at a table where my neighbor to my right was left-handed. He and I kept bumping elbows during the test, and the lighting was set for dining- not a three hour exam. Anyway, I got off to a slow start but finished strong. Now I had to wait six to eight weeks to get the results. I got a 74.5%. You needed 70 to pass, 85-94 to get a sub route, and 95 or higher to get your own route. Since the test was timed, I was at a disadvantage.

I was not done with potential teaching jobs, but the prospects were not great. About two weeks after the postal exam I received a call from the Wauwatosa School District. Apparently, Whitman Middle School was looking for a 7th grade social studies teacher. The only reason that I got a call from them was that my application was still on computer file with them. I had a brief "meet and greet" interview on Thursday June 16th. I did not get a chance to tell the interviewers that I had worked for their district as an at-risk teacher and that I was a finalist for an alternative education position at Wauwatosa East High School. Still, this sure beat the spring days of unsuccessfully applying for jobs with Best Buy and Home Depot. Having a mental illness like bipolar disorder makes it extremely difficult to garner the motivation. In my case I do not even know if my illness is on record. I am 99% sure that it is with the Milwaukee Public Schools. I have applied for positions with them and I get one-sentence rejection letters after having dynamite student teaching experiences. Discrimination really hurts. I used to wonder what it might be like to be a minority. I even used to try figuring out the mental toughness that slaves must have possessed during different historic eras. My disability is a quiet one that nobody really wants to talk about. There is a strong stigma. I praise the doctors and researchers that are putting in many hours to try finding cures and coping mechanisms for people with manic depression more commonly called bipolar disorder in the modern era.

If a teaching-related job or the postal service does not work out, then I will have to regroup in terms of finding employment. I used to be interested in a driving career. The Airport Connection in Milwaukee hires drivers to pick up and drop off travelers. They probably have something like that in El Paso, but I have problems with my left eye and am afraid to drive. I have not driven since the summer of 2012. Eye doctors have mixed views. Some think that I may have had a stroke because I have exotropia- a condition where the center of my eye leans towards the outside corner. Surgery could fix it, but it might revert back to the current condition. There is only one doctor in El Paso who can do the surgery, and he was not very empathetic towards me having bipolar disorder. Also, my medication would keep me from driving late at night and early in the morning when many people travel. Then again, I am not the best driver.

In September of 2003 I was pulled over by the Manitowoc Police while towing my boat home from northern Wisconsin. It had rained that day and was unseasonably chilly, so my clothes were still damp even when I got pulled over. Let's just say I was uncomfortable to say the least. I was driving in the left lane and was pulled over for swerving a tiny bit towards the grassy median. All I did was kick up some loose gravel, however, I did not know that the squad car was right behind me. The officer who pulled me over was a real hotshot. He summoned two other officers probably because he suspected me for driving under the influence of alcohol and/or drugs. Immediately he had me walking a straight line and balancing on one foot while alternating feet. I told all three police officers that I take Lithium Carbonate for bipolar disorder. They took me into the police station and had some guy draw my blood. It was about 9 o'clock and I was not even allowed to make a phone call. This was the first time that I was not read my Miranda Rights(the second time would be just over a year later when the Shorewood police beat the shit out of me).

Not able to call home, they put me in a cell and required me to wear prisoners' clothes. I slept there overnight on a steel platform with no pillow and fluorescent lights beaming down on me. The next morning I called my dad, and he came to pick me up and drive me back to our fishing van/boat trailer. I could tell that he was just as mad at the police as he was at me. We picked up the van and both of us headed back to our cottage less than forty-five minutes from Manitowoc. I ended up losing some points on my license. The fine was close to $300, and I had a good family friend attorney represent me. The points could have been greater since I was charged with inattentive driving.

What else was I up to post 2004 hospitalization? I still get depressed but never manic as long as I take my medication. I miss the highs. It is also very difficult to lose weight when depressed. This only exacerbated the depression. During the spring of 2005 I filed for bankruptcy. Law permitting, I erased close to $60,000 in medical debt. Also, my lawyer was so good that I did not lose anything- not even my IRA or individual retirement account policy. The money was supposed to be there for the future, for health concerns especially for my now wife and I.

I continued eating at Miss Latira's restaurant called Tres Hermanos. They have the best shrimp soup cocktail- even better than any I have tried in Texas. My ex-girlfriend picked up extra hours at some new Mexican restaurant by the airport so thankfully I do not have to see much of her and feel sorry for myself. One of the guys at the restaurant always comes up to my table, asks how I am doing, and tries finding out if anything was new in my life. He respected my loyalty- almost ten years straight of dining at their establishment.

In the summer of 2005 I was kind of at a crossroads in life. A major goal of mine was to get this book published, but I knew it would take time. I have asked Dr. Kay Redfield Jamison for assistance, but she may not even open my mail. Dr. Jamison has bipolar disorder, wrote the award-winning book "An Unquiet Mind," and works at Johns Hopkins University conducting psychiatric research. It became time after the splurging of writing in 2005 to start thinking about self-publishing. What an achievement it would be to publish a book! I wonder how many manic depressives actually sit down and write 100+ page books about their life experiences. I want to be an advocate for all of those that struggle with this illness and mental illness in general. Then there is the cost of publishing. I have not even begun to think about where I am going to get the funds to promote my work. It costs at least a few thousand dollars to self-publish. Money is tight since I had not sub-taught for close to a year.

Shades of Employment
and Brighter Prospects

AFTER A FEW stints of employment from 2006-2010, I picked up where I left off and began revising, editing, and making additions to this text starting in 2013. I had moved to Texas at the beginning of 2012. Since then I married the woman of my dreams and have been constantly coping with the absence of family and friends- most of which are back in Wisconsin and New York. My wife and I live with our two dogs: Gidget the Jack Russell and Harvee the Chihuahua.

During the spring of 2006 I applied for a camp counselor position in northwestern Wisconsin within the famous Crex Meadows Wildlife Area. I had a phone interview before getting hired. They liked the way that I possessed a teaching background. I got the nod and was hired. Camp started June 10th, but first I had to drive all the way to Minnesota's Audubon Center of the Northwoods for wilderness medical management training. This was a big-time test for me since I had not been in school for more than 6 years. There I met my camp director as well as one of the counselors. I missed passing the advanced wilderness first aid exam by three questions but still got the regular first responder license. With my head down, I went up to the camp director and told him I failed the exam. He told me not to sweat it. Nevertheless, I felt like a failure since I had always been great at taking tests.

I arrived at Crex Meadows Youth Conservation Camp on Saturday June 10th. This camp was designed for teenaged, high school at-risk youth meaning economically disadvantaged and/or taking medications. Before I could barely blink, I noticed that some of the youth were taking some of the same medications as me. It was kind of freaky. The summer schedule included three camp sessions spread out over the course of two months. We worked for the Department of Natural Resources clearing trails. A few times I got in trouble for flirting with female campers. I did not mean any harm and felt sorry I had opened my big mouth. I should have been flirting with our two female counselors. They were very nice. See, my camp director did not know that I was on medications. That would have impacted my chances of getting hired. If I had told him during the summer that I was taking meds, then they may have let me go.

There were a few fond memories that I have from the summer of 2006. First, I learned how to ride a horse. Mine was Mandy. She had shameful gas. Second, we camped along Lake Superior's northern shore. Third, I learned how to call owls and saw the "Birds of Prey" live exhibit in Minnesota. Finally, we did some hiking at Gooseberry Falls. In addition to these great memories, we saw two bears, many deer, learned about the Crex Meadows Wetlands, and got to have a fun movie night at the visitor center's theater towards the end of each of the three camp sessions. I regret not having kept in touch with the Crex Meadows staff.

I did get along well with our head male counselor at Crex. In between camp sessions we played some golf. I played so poorly because I had opened up to him and revealed my bipolar disorder to him. We enjoyed Chinese food dinners also in between sessions. He did treat me better after my making him aware of my illness. I was not looking for sympathy though. We had to share an A-frame cabin that summer, so we were kind of like brothers.

Depression hit me hard that summer because my then seven-year-old spring spaniel Cooper and I were apart for our first summer. Cooper had been through hell and back with me. Up until that summer he had been with me during down times never quick to judge me but always there with love. It's almost like I have not been fair to Cooper with all of my hospitalizations in 2000, 2001, 2002, 2004, and 2009. Still, I love him very much for being my faithful follower for his long life. Fortunately, my mom and Cooper came to visit me while I had a weekend off at camp. We drove to Minnesota's Audubon Center of the Northwoods and relaxed at the beach all day. I even took my mom to call owls. We were successful!

Upon returning home from camp I began looking for work. I targeted the 2006-07 school year. I interviewed for the hall monitor position at Rosenburg High School and got hired on the spot. It turned out to be a little of this and a little of that mostly high school and football game security, supervising the lunchroom, and a lot of substitute teaching. This increased my paychecks. I also coached 7th grade boys basketball over at the middle school. We won seven out of ten games and lost one of our games by one point to a team we had beaten by thirty the first time we played. My star player did not play during that loss, and one of my other key players could have won the game with a lay-up but he traveled.

The senior class gave me the nickname "Skittles" because I wore this multi-colored rugby shirt often. One particular art student went so far as to make a facial portrait out of Skittles candy wrappers. I was quite fond of the art teacher. She lived not too far from my parents' lake home with her six-year-old daughter. I asked her out a few different times to do something as mundane as go for a hike or in October go for a wagon ride out to the pumpkin patch with her daughter. Both times she said she could not due to conflicts. I gave up on her. Maybe I should have tried once more.

I only had one blemish on my record for the two years that I worked at Rosenburg High School. I jokingly asked a senior girl to go to a dance with me. She said yes but later reported me to the assistant principal. I had witnesses, but they were only students. They could back me up for this joke, and they were female so they had that perspective. The assistant principal, however, as well as the school's police liaison officer felt that I had crossed the line this time.

During most of the two years while at Rosenburg I had a crush on one of the math teachers. I used to fantasize about her when she passed my security desk in the front hall while on her way to check her mailbox. I ended up successfully inviting her to Milwaukee Brewers baseball and Marquette basketball games. She even came over for dinner twice when I was living with my folks. People just called her Wags because of her last name. Anyway, Wags led the Fellowship of

Christian Athletes at Rosenburg. We had meetings at 6 AM with live music, donuts, juice, and coffee. She helped me find God through scripture and Christian rock 'n roll. Currently, I find myself engaging in these activities while attending church most Sundays in Texas.

I felt as if Rosenburg had shortchanged me. For my first year I made $9.38/hour. For the second I made $9.76/hour. Both did not offer health insurance. The fact that I was sub teaching often made me think that I deserved benefits. After my first year I applied for a middle school paraprofessional position that would have given me a $2 raise but no benefits. I had no luck. A few weeks later I had the greatest opportunity. There was a social studies teacher opening at Rosenburg when one of the teachers decided to hang it up halfway through the school year. I eagerly waited and was hoping for an interview. I kept seeing people coming in dressed nice for an interview. The head principal came up to me in the hall and from behind me said, "Bryan, your name surfaced a few times this week." How fuckin cheap! I had been there one and one-half years and they could not even extend an interview. Even Wags was mad. Later that year I would have my setback of asking the female student to a dance. I was frustrated. Then it dawned on me. There probably was no doubt on the part of faculty and administrators of my suspected illness. They saw my mannerisms and behavior for close to two years. Why the discrimination though? I guess that Rosenburg personnel did not have faith in my abilities beyond that of the security/sub teacher role.

The most experienced hall monitor, Willa, always gave me a hard time. The "Wildebeast" acted like she was my boss and harped on me all of the time. Students might have joked around with me, but they would make fun of Willa for working at older than eighty years. She used to say to me, "Why are you so down all of the time?" I remember how upset my stomach would get hearing her bark her orders like Hitler. One day I barely made it to the restroom. She had upset my stomach, and I almost crapped in my pants.

My best friend from Rosenburg was a male math teacher who I will refer to as Captain Barbarosa due to his love for his thirty-four foot-sailboat and open water. He even looked like he was right out of

Disney's "Pirates of the Caribbean" with his grayish-black beard. We used to play golf after work and then get dinner. One of our favorite things to do was attend spring and fall Milwaukee Brewer baseball games. Captain Barbarosa was mighty good at scalping tickets. I'll never forget the time he landed two seats right behind home plate in the first row as long as we bought the couple's beer. They were playing the St. Louis Cardinals, and we got to see Albert Pujols up so close that night. It was also the night that Brewer relief pitcher and closer Trevor Hoffmann earned his 600th save.

Captain Barbarosa and I have done our fair share of fishing together. There would always be some beer accompanying us. I stuck to my one or two due to my medication regimen while he would exceed six. We preferred regular Leinenkugel's or Leinie Red. The captain had one of the best girlfriends. She would cook, clean, do his laundry, and keep him warm at night if you know what I mean. She has a beautiful home on a small, private lake in central Wisconsin. I have only been there once but had a good time fishing with Captain Barbarosa and his neighbor. Incidentally, I caught a 19 ½ inch white bass while on the Waupaca Chain of Lakes. We released it into his girlfriend's private lake. Another time the captain and his girlfriend visited my folks' lake cottage to fish for a long weekend. One time he was fighting by reeling in a largemouth bass when my dog Cooper jumped in and got the fish in his mouth. We were very lucky that good old Coop did not get any hooks in his mouth. From then on, Captain Barbarosa referred to Cooper as Dum-Dum. Unfortunately in my opinion, Captain Barbarosa broke up with his girlfriend. I hear that now he is happily married and spending his summers on his boat traversing most bays on Lake Michigan. We no longer keep in touch. I have his number, but he does not have mine.

With a shift in mindset, I began looking for a new job during the summer of 2008 two years after I began working at Rosenburg. Red Fox High School needed a special education aide. I seized the moment right at the very end of summer. After one day of orientation at Rosenburg, I quickly became part of the Red Fox staff. I was interviewed by the two most senior special education teachers. I looked forward to working with both. Best of all, I earned $2 more per hour and, more importantly, would now have health insurance and other benefits.

Red Fox High School was, in essence, no different than any of the most pressured Milwaukee Public high schools but was still considered a suburban school. In order to get my forty hours, I had to wake up early in the morning and open the school for future crowd control as well as stay after school to lead detention hall. This was not new to me because I had led detention at Rosenburg and man did that ever churn my stomach. The before school and after school duties gave me tons of stress. It took me a while, but I finally got the hang of detention. I did not allow anyone to come late. For a while, I worked with one of the female gym teachers in opening up the building but she was expecting a baby. Unfortunately, her replacement was an unreliable guy.

Both of my two years at Red Fox I worked part-time in the study skills resource room and part-time in students' regular education classes in small groups or one-on-one. My favorite teacher to work with was just down the hall from my office. She headed up the school's literacy program. We helped 9th and 10th graders read for comprehension with the ultimate goal for them being able to write a five paragraph essay with all of the essentials including introduction, thesis, body, and conclusion. One day while in the resource room at the end of the school day, one of the special education teachers took notice that I was not helping the three kids in the room. They had already told me that they did not need any help and wanted to work quietly. He brought it up the next day in the morning and made a big stink of it. This guy was judging me. He was the one that drank way too much, smoked weed and visited nudist colonies in the summertime. He must have told my boss because I lost my job on June 10, 2010 and have not worked for pay since then.

In 2009 from Valentine's Day until early August(almost 6 months) I dated a co-worker from Red Fox. She was thirteen years older, but I did not care at the time. Back in the days at Lincoln my mistress was twelve years older. Sometimes, having bipolar disorder, one tends to get lonely. I decided without thinking like a smart young man should that her offering sex and companionship was worth it. I would probably have a few thousand dollars more if not for this relationship since she made it clear that her town home rent would force me to pay for lunches, dinners, and entertainment. Nevertheless, it was a happy time. My weight was between 185 and 190, and I was in good shape. Work days went by faster. In the summer at the end of July/ early August I took her to New York to sightsee and visit relatives. Although probably for the best, she broke up with me one week after our New York trip. There was now a void in my life: frequent sex.

This 2009 girlfriend that I almost married was partially at my fault for my sexual obsessions. I was guilty too. This particular relationship was significant yet shallow as I would later find out due to the fact that it was highly sexual. One characteristic of bipolar disorder is increased sex drive. I mean we would fuck at least three to five times per week. I could have filled up a garbage bin with cum for all of the sex we had in that six month relationship. The one thing I regret is not capitalizing on her boob job from her post- divorce days. I wish I would have pulled out while fucking her missionary style and jacked off all over her huge tits.

She was older, but man could she ride cock. I estimate that I made her cum more than 75% of the time before I did, especially when she rode me cowgirl style. You should have seen her face when she was about to cum. What a self-serving prima donna. Still, I could be guilty of sin too. When I just felt selfish I would slide my modest-sized cock in her pussy missionary style- one sex position in which I do not last as long before cumming. Anyway, one time I wanted to do it doggie style. Here is the scenario. While she was talking to her eighteen-year-old daughter on the phone I was busy inserting my cock in her pussy from behind. That cunt told me that she could barely feel anything, so I thrusted faster and faster, pulled out and jacked off all over her ass. The reason why I write so vulgar about this girlfriend is that one: I have been disassociated from feeling some types of real love due to relationships that were highly sexual while growing up, two: I was sexually molested at a camp when I was 7 or 8 years old, and three: all she ever wanted was a sex partner, young sugar daddy being the nymphomaniac that she was. She most often initiated sex. I was busy watching "The Wrestler" one night at her house, and she said I will be waiting for you to fuck me when your movie is over. She even encouraged me to play with her asshole one time.

Nevertheless, she made me happy in the moment- you know mostly immediate gratification. In hindsight though, I was more like a willing sex slave. She would treat me only once for dinner on my birthday. My folks paid her airfare to New York and I funded the rest of the trip. I did not feel comfortable about it, but we had sex three or four times while staying at relatives' houses. I mean couldn't she hold off for a week. I was guilty then of immediate gratification. One week after our New York trip she broke up with me. I ended up in the hospital two weeks later and had to take medical leave for the fall. I sadly took the frustration of a broken relationship out on my family and spent almost one month at County. While there I mostly slept and felt depressed. I only worked at Red Fox for 1 ½ years. While taking medical leave that fall I burned all of my sick leave for the year. When I returned in the spring health reasons of depression forced me to be absent. This also contributed to my being let go in June. It is debatable as to whether there was any discrimination.

My First El Paso Visit

FROM THE SUMMER of 2010 until Thanksgiving I kept in touch with my future wife Sierra regularly. That was her Navy nickname when she worked in shoreline submarine detection of the Pacific Ocean while stationed at Pearl Harbor in the 1990's. Before serving at Pearl Harbor she succeeded at boot camp just outside of DisneyWorld in Orlando, FL. After that it was up the East Coast to Norfolk, VA. She was only there for a short while before being assigned to the California Coastline, but she did drive across the country in her shabby Nissan Sentra with, of course, stopping in El Paso to see family especially her father. Then, it was off to Monterrey, CA. Man, she really got to see some beautiful places while in the Navy. She even traveled to London, UK for two weeks, but Pearl Harbor ended up being her niche and there she monitored submarine activity of the Pacific Ocean. Her command was Navy Intelligence like my grandfather had been during WWII in the Air Force.

In 2011 we first met when I flew to El Paso for her holiday vacation from her special education teaching job. I experienced her great cooking, El Paso's fine dining, the local zoo with the sea lion show, and we went to two national parks including White Sands National Monument and Carlsbad Caverns National Park. My trip was memorable and convincing. We snuggled every night in that freezing house. Neither of us wanted to sleep alone. One of our framed pictures in the living room of our new house depicts Sierra and I in front of the Christmas tree at the airport. I had told my future wife a bonehead thought. I said to her, "You know it takes a while for two people to fall in love." I was back in El Paso for good in forty-five days. Unfortunately, I never met her mom because she died of a brain aneurysm when Sierra was just thirteen. Her father passed away from stroke complications at the age of seventy-six in July of 2011.

Sierra called me first crying profusely when this happened. She was a daddy's girl.

Sierra taught all day Monday through Friday leaving me at home all day: breeding grounds for depression as well as a potential writer's paradise. To intensify that depression, I had been away from family, my dog Cooper, and friends of close to forty years. I lived with my parents exclusively along with our dog Jonesy from 1987-1999 and Cooper from 1999-2011. I mean I just made a big move: flying down to Texas on January 10th on four days notice with a large suitcase full of clothes and some necessary items. My folks came down by car with Cooper in late March of 2012 and left him with us. He hated the Texas heat and could not swim anywhere. We vacationed in Wisconsin that summer and left Cooper there with my parents. He was definitely a Wisconsin dog full of love for all of the lakes and cooler spring and fall weather.

My mom mentioned to me that I like Latina women upon moving here for good. She may have even said that when she knew of my vacation plans to come to El Paso for the holidays in 2011. It turned out that my Mexican girlfriend prior to my 2004 manic episode fit that mold. Now the woman I am married to, love, and live with is of Mexican, Spanish, and Native-American ancestry. It is the culture and liveliness expressed in things like art and dancing not to mention the food that lures me in. Maybe I will not be a great teacher like my Latino classmate at UW-Milwaukee had predicted, but I am certainly married to one. This past semester she has been rising at 5 AM, leaving for school at 7 AM, and not returning home until 8 PM due to her homebound after-school commitments. My mom's father would have been proud. He passed away in 1989 before I was diagnosed. He served in US Air Force Intelligence during World War II using his fluency in six languages to inform Allied generals and higher-ups. He was learning Chinese the last two years of his life and had a full career as a Spanish and Latin teacher at the middle and high school levels. Both of my grandfathers served during World War II- the other in the Navy. He was stationed in the Pacific but never experienced combat.

From 2012 to Veterans Day of 2015 my wife and I lived in an old adobe house in San Elizario, TX. Half of our house was built in the 1640's. On November 15th of 2012 Sierra and I were married. It was the smallest of weddings. My parents and a longstanding psychiatrist family friend came down for the wedding. We had a brief ceremony at the Clint Courthouse. Depression fades in and out in my life. It can be chronic and is definitely medical as well as situational. My wife and I have had our difficult times together, but we always push forward and try to work things out even though my medications keep me down more than in an elevated mood state. For a while we attended support groups: mine for those with diagnoses and hers for family members of those with a diagnosis. There is a former UTEP professor in my support group that believes his office was "bugged" by some shadow government, so he and I can relate to each other. Like me he may be a bit crazy, but he did get earn his degree from the Massachusetts Institute of Technology(MIT). As I have stated before, bipolar disorder and other related mental illness generally first affect people in their late teens or early twenties and these are hard-driven, highly successful people up until that point in life.

My Health in El Paso

MY HEALTH IN El Paso is an interesting story. I decided to wait until I got Medicare and SSDI before choosing doctors. I stayed in touch with my Milwaukee psychiatrist via email and telephone. I saw my Milwaukee-based primary care physician during the summer of 2012 when we visited my home state. It took until the winter of 2013 to get new doctors in El Paso. I am seeing my second primary care physician, my second nephrologist or kidney doctor, and I have seen six psychiatric professionals. My weight gain, from 225 in 2012 to 260 today, has caused me to acquire sleep apnea. I have a sleep wellness doctor that prescribed a CPAP machine for easier breathing back in 2013.

I will try creating a clearer picture for what has taken place regarding my healthcare since moving to Texas. First, I have to backtrack a bit. Back when I lived in WI in 2011 I, along with the help from a representative, applied for Social Security Disability Insurance or SSDI. I was rejected. My father took it upon himself, being the attorney that he was, to write an essay to the Social Security Administration during the summer of 2012. I was accepted in late fall of that year and essentially became a Medicare card-carrying, SSDI recipient on December 7, 2012. I chose a Medicare Advantage Plan to cover the cost of prescriptions(I had been paying hundreds of dollars each month prior to this). I could finally see doctors in El Paso without paying up-the-ass. I found a primary care doctor and chose a mental health provider in his network.

My primary care doctor ordered bloodwork, and I was not caught off guard by the results. My creatinine levels were elevated indicating kidney failure, however, I knew this based on conclusions from my WI primary care doctor. I would need a nephrologist or kidney disease doctor to treat my chronic interstitial nephritis or Stage 3 kidney disease. It was believed that the Lithium Carbonate over time caused this damage. Amazingly, I have been poked with needles probably close to 500 times in my life because I had been on Lithium for twenty-three straight years. I have scar tissue, and it is difficult for phlebotomists to access healthy veins. As a result, sometimes I have major bruises and I look like a heroin addict. The first nephrologist that I saw drew blood again and then, out of the blue one day without any appointment, had his staff call me to set up a biopsy. I switched to a new kidney doctor and soon also found a new primary care doctor.

My first psychiatrist was knowledgeable, but her staff did not understand how to bill me correctly. It was headache after headache. Worse yet, my wife and I waited for up to 3 ½ hours in the waiting room for appointments. She gave good advice, but I needed someone more generous with his/her time. I found a great guy who cared for me for close to three years at two different clinics. The only drawback was that he did not want to take me off of the Lithium. When he ended his time as my caregiver I then had to go to appointments all the way on the West side. There I would see four professionals over the course of less than two years. Their staff was rude, incomplete, and innacurate with their computers, but one physician's assistant had the courage to recommend taking me off of Lithium. I replaced it with a different mood stabilizer in late November of 2016. While Lithium is processed in the kidneys, my new mood stabilizer is processed in the liver. Today I have far fewer blood draws each year!

Seeing doctors on the West side of El Paso is a royal pain in the ass since we live in the southeast section of El Paso County. The reason why it is so bad stems from the major traffic and construction. My current mental health provider now and all of my other doctors are located on the East side. My mental health provider specializes in psychotherapy and treating veterans with post-traumatic stress syndrome(PTSS), which my doctor says I suffer from. Night sweats, talking in sleep, yelling in sleep, falling out of bed, and running down the hallway in the middle of the night and falling in pain on a few occasions have led to this diagnosis. So now I guess I am bipolar, have

PTSS, and have some obsessive- compulsions like worrying until my stomach hurts about going to b ood draws and getting worked-up over doctor appointments.

My doctor visits vary in frequency of appointments. I see my primary care doctor twice each year and as needed, my kidney doctor three times each year, my psychiatric professional six times per year, my "talk" therapy will begin in February of 2018, and my sleep apnea doctor twice each year. As you can see it is all a bit complicated.

Stage 3 kidney disease is serious in that if it becomes Stage 4 then the doctor will often put the patient on dialysis and recommend a transplant. Luckily, my kidney function(measured by the creatinine in my blood)has remained very stable since moving here six years ago. The levels are elevated but have not fluctuated much. My kidney doctor appointment on December 28, 2017 showed results that I am actually improving to a small degree.

An ongoing issue has occurred with my left eye. In the late spring of 2012 we went to get our licenses renewed at motor vehicles division. I kept my WI driver's license but I needed a TX state ID. I noticed in my picture that my left eye was off centered. The center of my eyeball reverts to the outside corner of my eye in a condition called exotropia. I have not driven since August of 2012. My wife has pretty much been my chauffeur for the past 5 years. I looked into possible surgery. Only one doctor in El Paso can perform it. His assistant gave me a comprehensive eye exam and wrote down all of my psychiatric and regular medications back in November of 2015. My dad and I must have waited for three hours just to be seen.

At that time I was still taking Lithium. This mood stabilizer along with the anti-psychotic Halopericol causes tremors or shaking in the hands. I had problems with the tremors ever since moving to TX, but especially that day. The doctor tried fitting me for prism lenses that might be able to cure my eye. He concluded that I needed surgery and that it may only be temporarily successful as the eye could revert back. He said I would be under general anesthesia especially since I had that "funky thing" going on with my hands. I could not believe he said that.

He must have just disregarded my chart and list of medications. Pretty insensitive I concluded. If he ever does the surgery, then he will need to make two cuts in the left eye muscle and one in the right. I would have to wear a patch for one week over my left eye. I had no plans of rushing into this.

Our Bipolar Marriage

BIPOLAR DISORDER IS marked by a life full of serious, sometimes abrupt mood swings. Our marriage has also been a bit rocky and unstable. I have sought advice from friends in their 40's up until 80's to try in improving our marriage. We are steadily doing better. She can be like a bull whereas I can be her rhino counterpart. We clash sometimes and both have alpha personalities meaning once our mind is set on something, then it is difficult to change it.

I have to admit I have said hurtful things to my wife, and I conclude that I probably initiate them more than her. She is no saint though. My pastor tells me that I should worship my wife and have her as my central focus in life. This brings to mind scripture related to our personalities. "Stupid people always think they are right. Wise people listen to advice. When a fool is annoyed he quickly lets it be known. Smart people will ignore an insult"(Proverbs 12: 15-16). Often my wife and I both think we are right. I believe the key is not to let things escalate. "Any fool can start arguments; the honorable thing is to stay out of them"(Proverbs 20:3).

Your typical weekday during the school year culminated with me asking my wife how her day went, how were the kids, and if anything exciting happened that day that I would find interesting. She is an autism specialist within the special education department. I used to volunteer there but it became too political and there were cliques or smaller social groups that were kind of exclusive.

I sometimes cook in the crock pot or do prep work for dinner when home, but it's the dogs that benefit by my staying home. They get to go out three or four times instead of having to hold their bladders for ten hours. Gidget, the female Jack Russell Terrier, is a rescue dog just like Harvee our Chihuahua. Gidget turns 11 in January while Harvee turned 3 last September. We found Harvee wrapped in pajamas lying in the street at our old house with a bullet on his collar. Gidget was going to be left in the canals in winter as a puppy, but my wife rescued her. They love sunbathing at our new home in the backyard especially on spring and fall days. We pamper them by not allowing them to stay out long in the summer heat. I volunteered at the San Eli elementary school up the block from our old house from spring of 2013 to fall of 2014. Then I began volunteering at my wife's school mostly in physical education. Towards the end(spring 2017)I worked in her classroom helping to get the kids ready for state standardized testing. For the 2016 and 2017 school years I was the top volunteer in terms of hours logged although not necessarily most valuable. Those ladies work so hard every day that they come in!

At the San Eli elementary school the kids were taught military-like training by coach and his assistant. It was hard work for them, but the coaches made it fun except for when they had the kids run around the track when it was close to 100 degrees. To this day I remain friends with the coach. We have shared movies, and I have even purchased some off of Amazon for him: funny movies like "Revenge of the Nerds" and serious ones such as "Life is Beautiful."

I began my volunteering duties in the fall of 2014 at my wife's school. I worked with two male coaches. One of them always has a smile on his face even when he is mad about something. He is more laid back while the other coach was more of a disciplinarian. He was relocated to a school right up the road after a year or two. I provided a sense of humor for the kids while still being demanding like the coaches. The new coach's assistant looked like rock star Joan Jett and played cool music when the kids were outside, and both of them played cool music indoors.

The first two coaches at my wife's school enjoyed discussing movies during lunch. My favorite is the first "Men in Black" and the more laid back coach and I agreed it was a great movie while the other coach argued that it was only a good movie. Anyway, we have been imitating Edgar the alien ever since 2014 and watching video clips. Coach's favorite line occurs at the end when Edgar's spaceship is shot down by Tommy Lee Jones and Will Smith. Edgar says to them, "It don't matter. In fact in a few seconds you won't even be matter." My favorite part takes place in the morgue when Edgar says, "You ever pull wings off of a fly? You care to see a fly get even?" I have not made many friends here in TX, but I consider the two coaches more than just acquaintances. One is a daddy for the second time in 3 years while the other is assistant varsity baseball coach at a large high school. Both are obviously very busy, but they do sometimes find some time to spend with my wife and I. Both are married, and my wife and I enjoy their company.

Faith and Spiritual Life

MY FAVORITE PHRASE to hear when going to worship at Reaching Your Generations Pentecostal Church is "En el nombre de Jesus"(meaning in the name of Jesus). We used to go to a mega-church called Abundant Living Faith Center before moving on to our much smaller, family church where the congregation is trying to grow. Both places have great praise and worship music with live bands. My wife even sometimes plays the sax along with vocalists, guitarists, drummers, and keyboardists. Reaching Generations started in a garage five years ago. We have an international traveling pastor from Dallas that guides and supports us. Services are Wednesday nights and Sunday mornings. Although our pastors would like us to worship at both services we generally try making it five or six times each month. Wednesday nights are too difficult for my wife most often except in summer and during holiday breaks. Our pastor tells us that he loves us and wants all of us to be church leaders. He understands my financial difficulty and does not badger me to give money. I have given before. Our congregation ranges from anywhere from five to forty for any given service. I respect my wife for the role faith plays in her life and it has impacted me.

Reaching Generations focuses on healing, restoring relationships such as family and friends, and definitely restoring marriages. The very first book of the Old Testament says, "It is not good for man to live alone. I will make him a suitable companion"(Genesis 2:18). Maintaining relationships is just as important as restoring them. "Be always humble, gentle and patient. Show your love by being tolerant of one another"(Ephesians 4:2-3). Furthermore, the Bible talks about forgiveness. "Get rid of all bitterness, passion, and anger. No more shouting or insults, no more hateful feelings of any sort. Instead, be kind and tender-hearted to one another, as God has forgiven you through Christ"(Ephesians 4:31-32).

So humbleness, forgiveness, and good open lines of communication are necessary in maintaining and restoring relationships and marriages. "Everyone must be quick to listen, but slow to speak and slow to become angry"(James 1:19). We have discovered that marriage is a work in progress hopefully. Many family friends have advised that marriage has its ups and downs. The foundations have been laid and now is time for commitment.

My wife and I have an angel named Carolina in our lives whom I keep in touch with a few days each week. She is my former boss as the former volunteer coordinator at my wife's elementary school. Carolina is the epitome of a good Samaritan always serving the less fortunate by taking friends and acquaintances to doctor appointments and visiting nursing homes. She has a lot on her plate, especially since she is also a caregiver to her younger brother who lives with her. A former teacher and assistant principal, Carolina has encouraged me to take on a more active role in education given my background. She has even offered to drive me to potential interviews. I am reluctant though because I have lost education jobs, and working in a school is just another institution with a social and political hierarchy. Both Carolina and my wife, most importantly, have leaned on me when it comes to faith and spirituality as well as an acceptance and stewardship for God. Losing friends to old age and seeing friends and family in pain has been common for Carolina in the past year. Still, she just keeps on charging forward like the "little drummer boy" bangs his drum. With aging comes loss, but it is never easy to cope with or accept.

Epilogue

MY MARINE CORPS boss from Lincoln Park Golf Course deserves a purple heart and/or congressional medal of honor. He took me under his wing because he saw that we shared much in common: that being PTSD or sometimes now called PTSS for everything that happened so quickly in Washington DC back in 1993 seven months after the inauguration of the Clinton/Gore Administration and two seasons before the Republican Contract for America. There were three major lowlights. The events leading up to my encounter with the dean of the Washington Semester Program, the principal for Milwaukee Public Schools(MPS)that interfered with me, my studies at UW-Milwaukee, and the many female relationships that ended fairly abruptly are just to name a few. The sexual relationships lacked substance. It was only my experiences with my family, friends, my golf course boss and ultimately my current wife that have kept me from aimlessly wandering the streets homeless like many people who are veterans and/or have a mental illness.

The congressional candidate that I volunteered for in Milwaukee back in 1992 has since been in the Governor of Wisconsin's Cabinet, has been appointed to numerous foundations, played a key role in the recent election of Milwaukee's County Executive, and still managed to practice law and help raise a family. He was recently divorced.

You know how there are six degrees of separation between the average person and world leaders. Well, this guy dined with the likes of Bill Bradley, Al Gore, Bill and Hillary Clinton, Barack Obama, and a whole slew of members of the Republican Party including Congressman James Sensenbrenner of southeastern Wisconsin. As a loyal centrist Democrat, he has been at odds sometimes with the conservative-leaning Foley and Lardner law firm. Today he is dead. He passed away in his early 50's after working out from a brain aneurysm much like that of my wife's mother's cause of death. I have so many questions that I need to ask him, but he is gone. I want some explanations too(and justice)because I encounter flashbacks on a regular basis. My psychiatric provider has no doubt that I suffer from trauma. You do not have to be military to live with post-traumatic stress disorder(PTSD). I am getting bags under my eyes like Bill Clinton from my interrupted, inadequate sleep.

The impetus for finishing this book and embarking on the endeavor of becoming published was instilled in me during the summer and early fall of 2017 when I began contacting members of the US Congress. These included Senator Lindsey Graham(R-SC), Senator John Cornyn(R-TX), indirectly Senator Ted Cruz(R-TX), indirectly Senator John McCain(R-AZ), Congress James Sensenbrenner(R-WI), and Congressman Will Hurd(R-TX).

I spoke with various staff members, sent resumes, gave detailed background information, wrote an email to Bush 43's retirement office, and urged the National Governor's Association along with the Foley and Lardner law firm to squeeze the Illinois state legislature and start to alleviate their tax problems(Interestingly, a great amateur golfer and current Foley and Lardner real estate director now is the Masters Chairman at Augusta National for the first of the men's pro golf majors in April). I also proposed national park reform to create jobs for teens and seniors especially as well as veterans, and among others suggested that Houston get on the horn after Harvey and the following hurricanes to get SC Johnson, a Racine, WI based family, private company to donate plastic bottles of insect repellent to the affected areas for residents and clean-up, rebuilding workers. I even said former Dallas Cowboy Quarterback Tony Romo was from Racine, WI originally so he could probably swing the deal with SC Johnson along with some pressure from the Wisconsin delegation. Finally, in messages to Senator Ted Cruz(R-TX) and others I discussed monetary policy and said Dow at least 23,500 by December 31st. All markets have improved. Now it is time to establish programs for the less fortunate to establish Individual Retirement Accounts(IRAs)and balanced, modest portfolios. I will have to dip into my IRA for personal health reasons as well as to purchase a computer to finish this book and pay for the publishing fees.

I encourage moderate Republicans who believe that global climate change is a major issue affecting the US and entire world to run for president in the future. Trump may or may not get his 2nd term. Many of the midterm congressional elections are in states that Trump carried handily, and there still are more Republican governors. I have offered my elected officials here in TX my time and even been willing to do contract work on prison reform and its link in rehabilitating prisoners under the authority of the Bureau of Alcohol, Tobacco, and Firearms(ATF)and even possibly the Drug Enforcement Administration(DEA). I want to be behind the scenes having an impact or influence over policymaking not as an elected official like once before. That's a ballgame only for the special few with skeletons in their closets. Speaking of ballgames, I even suggested to a select group of congressional members who might be a good nominee for the next associate Supreme Court Justice. I know of a former legal expert in major league baseball who was also a West Point graduate and served during combat in Vietnam. He practiced law as a litigator for Foley and Lardner in Milwaukee and now is semi-retired practicing in New York City.

I wanted to make another comment on white collar crime and insider trading. In one of his State of the Union speeches(and I do not remember which), President Obama called on members of Congress to stop participating or engaging in insider trading. Campaign war chests due to the incumbency effect, political action committees(PACs)and Superpacs, and lawyer-lobbyists making ¾ of a million dollars each year all have influence that takes away from who government was supposed to serve: the American people such as regular, everyday taxpaying citizens. A member of Congress' $300,000+ salary can be increased 10x, 20x or even 30x over by unfair financial practices such as insider trading. I believe that I was a victim of this in late August of 1993. I had to learn the lesson the hard way that "All politics are local" and that "Politics makes for strange bedfellows" as stated in Hedrick Smith's "The Power Game."

I have come to the conclusion that those with integrity deserve to be acknowledged. By this I mean the PGA TOUR or professional golfers association. I am getting old so I follow the Champions or senior tour as much if not more than the regular tour. I like watching the ladies too. They salute the flag and honor the military on the last couple of holes of most if not all tournaments. While warming up to compete there is the MarketWatch ticker in their view showing how the DOW, NASDAQ, and S&P are doing. These guys are the bedrock foundation of support for American and multinational corporations. In former Ryder Cup and President's Cup events the US team used to fly overseas 900 mph on the Concorde. They get a bit pampered, but they deserve it by playing by the rules of the game. Sure, most of them live in the South and feel secure with featured theme parks like DisneyWorld and DisneyLand nearby as well as the majority of the military bases- not to mention the great weather. Still, there is Steve Stricker and Jerry Kelly of Wisconsin. Look at their career earnings and you may be surprised. A snowbird from the Midwest originally heads the Bible study group on the Champions Tour and now calls Scottsdale, AZ home without ever forgetting where he came from. Other great players hail from the Northeast where they grew up. These PGA TOUR players do not forget their roots and are some of the more humble men I know. By the way, I finished writing this book on Tiger Woods' birthday. My oh my what he has meant for the game of golf. God bless him. I would have been a good PGA TOUR employee!

The majority of the pro golfers also give back to local communities each week as well as national foundations such as St. Jude Children's Hospital and Special Olympics to name a few. The late Arnold Palmer established his own children's hospital in Orlando and the great Jack Nicklaus makes a point of promoting children's causes as well as that of the less fortunate. Young and older pros support the First Tee Foundation. Sure, they get tax write-offs for their financial contributions but just think of all the time they focus on many of the causes such as medical conditions.

I try giving to charity, but this is difficult without a sustainable income. When the seriousness of my kidney disease surfaced I decided to quit my monthly contributions to the Wounded Warrior Project or WWP. The reason why I had chosen to support WWP was because I have seen and lived amongst military veterans with mental illnesses during my many hospital stays and in doctor's waiting rooms. I may have never shot a gun in combat or been shot at, but my doctor has concluded that I suffer from ongoing trauma in my mind. As noted before, I currently see four doctors as well as a psychotherapist. The copays and prescriptions can get expensive, so I had to make the decision to halt my WWP monthly payments. In addition to this former charity, I am a member of Coca-Cola's mycokerewards.com. Over the past three years I have donated points found on codes under beverage caps and on 12-packs and cases. My wife and I gave up soda except for Coke's versions of ginger ale and root beer, but we do drink sugar free Powerade. When I go for walks I often look for Coke caps, and I have friends giving me their codes. Why do I do this? The points go to noteworthy causes like the American Red Cross, the USO, St. Jude's Children's Hospital, Children's Miracle Network, the Boys and Girls Clubs of America, Special Olympics, and the National Parks Foundation. I feel I am doing my part given my means of income.

A Variety of Readers(Editors)

I have had seven or eight peer editors for my book including my wife, my two best friends(One has been a UPS driver for 26 years while the other is a supervisory engineer for the tractor line with Case New Holland and formerly worked for Cummins Engines), a West Point graduate engineer whose parents were both in the Central Intelligence Agency(CIA), a former nuclear engineer Navy Officer who worked in finance for a goliath utilities company, an IT systems technician and researcher at the top of his field, former chief legal counsel for Northwestern Mutual Life Insurance(NML), and an active church member from Whitefish Bay who serves as a spiritual mentor and, despite having bipolar disorder for his adult life, worked as an actuary for NML for close to 40 years.

In addition, excerpts from my book have been read by US Senator and Majority Whip John Cornyn(R-TX)who serves on the Intelligence, Judiciary, and Finance Committees as well as Congressman Will Hurd(R-TX)who serves on committees such as Cybersecurity, Intelligence, and Oversight. Mr. Hurd worked in the private sector in cybersecurity after a decade-plus career as a CIA officer in the Middle East.

My chief editor of the first manuscript, the first 80%, was my family and psychiatrist friend who in the past ten years has managed to publish two books. My mother also read the original manuscript but much has been added since 2005.

www.ingramcontent.com/pod-product-compliance
Lightning Source LLC
Chambersburg PA
CBHW032105080426
42733CB00006B/419